E　　　　D0358085

WITHDRAWN

JULIUS CAESAR

The RSC Shakespeare

Edited by Jonathan Bate and Eric Rasmussen
Chief Associate Editors: Jan Sewell and Will Sharpe
Associate Editors: Trey Jansen, Eleanor Lowe, Lucy Munro,
Dee Anna Phares, Héloïse Sénéchal

JULIUS CAESAR

Textual editing: Eric Rasmussen
Introduction and Shakespeare's Career in the Theatre: Jonathan Bate
Commentary: Erin Sullivan and Héloïse Sénéchal
Scene-by-Scene Analysis: Esme Miskimmin
In Performance: Karin Brown (RSC stagings) and Peter Kirwan (overview)
The Director's Cut (interviews by Jonathan Bate and Kevin Wright):
Edward Hall, David Farr and Lucy Bailey

Editorial Advisory Board

Gregory Doran, Chief Associate Director,
Royal Shakespeare Company
Jim Davis, Professor of Theatre Studies, University of Warwick, UK
Charles Edelman, Senior Lecturer, Edith Cowan University,
Western Australia
Lukas Erne, Professor of Modern English Literature,
Université de Genève, Switzerland
Jacqui O'Hanlon, Director of Education, Royal Shakespeare Company
Akiko Kusunoki, Tokyo Woman's Christian University, Japan
Ron Rosenbaum, author and journalist, New York, USA
James Shapiro, Professor of English and Comparative Literature,
Columbia University, USA
Tiffany Stern, Professor and Tutor in English, University of Oxford, UK

The RSC Shakespeare

WILLIAM SHAKESPEARE

JULIUS CAESAR

Edited by
Jonathan Bate and Eric Rasmussen

Introduced by Jonathan Bate

Macmillan

© The Royal Shakespeare Company 2011

Published by arrangement with Modern Library, an imprint of The Random House Publishing Group, a division of Random House, Inc.

All rights reserved. No reproduction, copy or transmission of this publication may be made without written permission.

No portion of this publication may be reproduced, copied or transmitted save with written permission or in accordance with the provisions of the Copyright, Designs and Patents Act 1988, or under the terms of any licence permitting limited copying issued by the Copyright Licensing Agency, Saffron House, 6–10 Kirby Street, London EC1N 8TS.

Any person who does any unauthorised act in relation to this publication may be liable to criminal prosecution and civil claims for damages.

'Royal Shakespeare Company', 'RSC' and the RSC logo are trade marks or registered trade marks of The Royal Shakespeare Company.

The right of Jonathan Bate and Eric Rasmussen to be identified as the authors of the editorial apparatus to this work by William Shakespeare has been asserted by them in accordance with the Copyright, Designs and Patents Act 1988.

Published 2010 by
MACMILLAN PUBLISHERS LTD
registered in England, company number 785998, of Houndmills, Basingstoke, Hampshire RG21 6XS.
Companies and representatives throughout the world

ISBN-13 978-0-230-28410-4 paperback

This book is printed on paper suitable for recycling and made from fully managed and sustained forest sources. Logging, pulping and manufacturing processes are expected to conform to the environmental regulations of the country of origin.

A catalogue record for this book is available from the British Library.

10   9   8   7   6   5   4   3   2   1
20   19   18   17   16   15   14   13   12   11

Printed in China

CONTENTS

INTRODUCTION

ELIZABETHAN POLITICS AND THE ROMAN EXAMPLE

Sir Francis Walsingham, Queen Elizabeth I's Secretary of State, recommended the study of history with an eye to its contemporary applications: 'in the reading of histories as you have principally to mark how matters have passed in government in those days, so have you to apply them to these our times and states and see how they may be made serviceable to our age'. It was in this spirit that Sir Thomas North produced his translation of Plutarch's *Lives of the Noble Grecians and Romans*, the main source for Shakespeare's dramatizations of the events leading to the deaths of Julius Caesar, Brutus and Cassius, Marcus Antonius and his beloved Cleopatra, and Caius Martius Coriolanus. *Julius Caesar*, performed at the Globe theatre in 1599, was the first of the three plays in which Shakespeare followed Plutarch closely in exploring key moments of transition in the history of Rome.

Unlike Plutarch, though, Shakespeare begins with the people rather than the politicians. The common tradesmen are taking a day's unofficial holiday in celebration of the return of the conquering Caesar. But the victory in question is not an imperial one: Julius Caesar has defeated another Roman general, Pompey the Great, in a civil war. The play will end with renewed civil war. Elizabethan political culture was much exercised by the dangers of, on the one hand, the civil strife concomitant upon uncertainty over the transmission of power and, on the other, the potential for tyranny if too much power were invested in an individual. In the opening scene the Tribunes – official spokesmen for the popular will – are worried that the military supremo is proving too popular. They demand the removal of the tokens honouring Caesar that have been draped over the statues in the Capitol. We learn a little

later that for their pains in doing so they have been 'put to
silence'. This kind of detail lends support to Orson Welles'
influential 1930s production of the play with its jackbooted Caesar
and its handling of Antony's funeral oration as something out of a
Nuremberg Rally.

We should, however, be cautious in fully endorsing such a
reading. The conspirators are not disinterested idealists. Brutus, the
most thoughtful of them, does not initially focus his fears on
Caesar's ambitions; such a prospect is conjured into him by Cassius'
cunning rhetoric. '[T]he quarrel', remarks Brutus in soliloquy, 'Will
bear no colour for the thing he is'. He only persuades himself to join
the conspirators by 'fashioning' the argument that the act of
crowning Caesar might itself be the egg that, when hatched, would
unleash tyranny upon the state. The historical irony for Rome, and
the personal tragedy for Brutus, is that the conspiracy itself proves
to be the thing that divides the city and lets slip the dogs of a civil
war that only ceases at the end of *Antony and Cleopatra*, when
Octavius becomes Augustus and ushers in the imperial phase of
Rome's history.

For over a thousand years, Rome was the city of the world. The
Romans ruled the greatest empire that had ever been seen. Even
after its decline and fall, the name of Rome lived on for centuries by
providing the western world with models of excellence in every
dimension of human life from military technology to political
sophistication to theory of moral character to cultural glories such as
architecture and epic poetry.

Shakespeare's England was a small, vulnerable, upstart nation
near the northwestern edge of the known world. When Queen
Elizabeth came to the throne, the country was in a state of near
psychotic self-division as a result of her father's break from that
latter-day Roman empire, the universal Catholic church. But in the
course of her reign, aristocrats, intellectuals, seamen, poets and
theatre people forged an amazingly bold new vision: that one day,
their tiny island-nation might become a second Rome. They laid
out the building blocks for the future. Naval power saw off the
might of Spain and planted the name of the Virgin Queen on

distant shores. Politicians honed a system of checks and balances between the two houses of parliament and the monarchy – a system based on the Roman model of senators, tribunes and emperor, but with a more flexible legal system, based on common law 'precedent' rather than a fixed code of rules. Educators opened grammar schools for the middle classes, steeping the future administrators of nation and empire in both the Latin language and the Roman character of firm backbone and stiff upper lip (known technically as Stoicism). And Shakespeare's actors staged epic dramas in which they told the heroic history both of their own nation and of the Romans who were their ideal. So it was that when Britannia came to rule the waves in the eighteenth and nineteenth centuries, Shakespeare's *Julius Caesar* was central to the education and character-formation of aristocrat, politician and imperial civil servant alike. Mark Antony's great speech that sways the popular will – 'Friends, Romans, countrymen, lend me your ears' – was learned by rote in school and analysed as the exemplary piece of persuasive oratory (not least because of its witty trope of denying its own force – 'I am no orator').

The year 1599, when the play was written and performed, was a time of intense political debate. The second Spanish Armada had been broken up by bad weather two years before, so superpower rivalry was no longer the most pressing issue of the day. The problem now was how to deal with a country that was apparently harbouring rebels and terrorists who were a threat to the new world order. That country was Ireland. Was the answer negotiation or brute force?

The argument that prevailed might be described as the neo-conservative position. It went something like this. England stood on the threshold of greatness. Having seen off Spain, it had the potential to become the greatest empire in the modern world. And so to the classic conservative move: look to the past in order to understand the present. The greatest empire in history was that of the ancient Romans. But Rome hadn't been built in a day. It had only achieved its power by building a mighty army and developing military technology of unprecedented sophistication. Above all, it needed a military genius, an all-conquering general who could hold whole continents in the palm of his hand. His name, of course, was Julius Caesar.

The leading exponent of this position was the Earl of Essex. He sponsored the authorship of historical works and translations of classical texts that supported his ideals of Roman virtue and fortitude. He offered himself to Queen Elizabeth as a modern Julius Caesar. In March 1599 he set off for Ireland at the head of a mighty army. In the autumn he skulked back to the queen's court in London, having ignominiously failed to defeat the Irish rebels. Superior firepower could not deal with the guerrilla tactics of the insurgents. Shakespeare's play was written in the fearful interim between the first motion against the insurrection and the realization of the hideous dream of failure.

Essex's image of himself as Julius Caesar went to his head. His Rubicon moment came eighteen months later when, 'assisted by sundry Noblemen and Gentlemen' (Shakespeare's patron, the Earl of Southampton, among them), he marched against the queen herself, vainly imagining that the people of London would flood into the streets and offer him the crown. He was executed for his pains.

Shakespeare had a very different take on his material from that of Essex. He was fascinated by the assassination of Julius Caesar and its aftermath because this was the period in Roman history that asked the most fundamental questions about politics: does authority belong to the people, to an individual ruler, or to an abstraction called the 'state'? What is the most effective form of government – a monarchy, an empire, an oligarchy, a republic?

At the beginning of the play, the long-established Roman republic, with its system of checks and balances (senators representing the patricians and tribunes the plebeians), is in crisis. If Caesar is not stopped, democracy will be destroyed. But are the men who try to stop him acting out of duty to the state or personal ambition? And what happens once the knife has gone in? Chaos, civil war, and then the events of the play's sequel, *Antony and Cleopatra*, in which there is a failed attempt to divide rule between three men and then the rise to power of a new Caesar, Octavius, who would later be called Augustus, the inaugurator of the imperial phase of Roman history.

Despite the fact that he was writing under Elizabeth, a queen-emperor who saw herself as another Augustus, and despite the apparent approval of Essex's Irish expedition that he worked into the prologue of *Henry V* at exactly the time he was writing *Julius Caesar*, Shakespeare seems to have been genuinely sceptical about the imperial project associated with the name of Caesar. At the same time, he was horrified by the idea of mob rule, as witness the scene when Cinna the poet is lynched because he happens to share a name with one of the conspirators.

THE ROMAN PHILOSOPHY

The character who invites particular sympathy is Brutus, guardian of republican values, as he wrestles with the question of whether to be or not to be a conspirator. Cassius espouses the philosophy of Epicurus, who believed that the gods do not intervene in human affairs: what will be will be, and so there is no need to pay attention to omens and auguries. From this philosophy it is only a short step to that of Machiavelli – might is right and there is no such thing as a moral order. Brutus, by contrast, is portrayed as a Stoic, a philosophy associated with the idea of duty and the cultivation of mental fortitude as a shield against the vicissitudes of fortune. In each case, though, experience proves the philosophy insufficient. When news comes that Portia is dead, Brutus is 'sick of many griefs'. Cassius replies: 'Of your philosophy you make no use, / If you give place to accidental evils'. It is much harder in practice than in theory to rise above the accidents and chances that life throws at us.

Stoicism generally argued that adversity should be faced, not escaped, and that suicide was therefore not the answer. That is why Brutus considers that the austere moralist Cato let the side down when he killed himself: 'Even by the rule of that philosophy / By which I did blame Cato for the death / Which he did give himself'.

But the proposition is soon belied by the unfolding action. Unable to bear the thought of the shame of being led through Rome a prisoner, Brutus takes himself the way of Cato.

Cassius is also forced into the discovery that philosophical theories have a way of being belied by events. When foreboding ravens, crows and kites hover in place of mighty eagles over his army, he interprets the change as a divine sign and is therefore forced to modify his Epicurean belief that the gods do not speak to mortals: 'You know that I held Epicurus strong / And his opinion: now I change my mind / And partly credit things that do presage'. 'Partly credit' is good: he has not entirely renounced the Epicurean scepticism about omens and auguries.

One of the most significant manifestations of the Roman influence on sixteenth-century ideas was the philosophy known as neo-Stoicism: as Cicero and Seneca had wrestled with the role of the intellectual in an age of instability or tyranny, so thinkers in the age of Shakespeare sought to reconcile the Stoic idea of indifference to fortune with the Christian conception of divine providence. For a self-consciously intellectual dramatist such as Fulke Greville, friend of Sir Philip Sidney and lord over Stratford-upon-Avon, neo-Stoicism was the foundation for both a theory of drama and a political position. Shakespeare wasn't like that; he was too nimble on his feet and wary of his back to sign up to any philosophical or political code. But the fact that his plays are the exact opposite of propaganda does not mean that they lack philosophy or politics: *Julius Caesar* spoke to the turmoil of AD 1599 just as much as to that of 44 BC.

A clock strikes, men wear doublets rather than togas, night-watchmen patrol and there are references to handkerchiefs: such purposeful anachronisms reveal that Shakespeare was a 'modern-dress' dramatist, making the past speak to the present. To what degree should political power be concentrated in a single leader? Is the democratic process strong enough to withstand a potential tyrant or are there times when direct action on the street is the only possible course of action? Can we trust politicians to serve the people rather than their own interests? In addressing such questions, the play remains alive and full of troubling force in the twenty-first century.

Shakespeare is always interested in how words are confounded by deeds, how political and philosophical positions collapse under the pressure of action and circumstance. In the end, *Julius Caesar* is a play about decision-making and conscience as much as it is an exploration of politics and of Roman value systems.

Shakespeare must have had the heavy folio of North's Englished Plutarch open on his desk as he wrote. Read the 'Life of Marcus Brutus' therein and you see the raw materials on which the dramatist's imagination set to work:

> Now Brutus (who knew very well that for his sake all the noblest, valiantest, and most courageous men of Rome did venture their lives) weighing with himself the greatness of the danger, when he was out of his house he did so frame and fashion his countenance and looks that no man could discern he had anything to trouble his mind. But when night came that he was in his own house, then he was clean changed. For, either care did wake him against his will when he would have slept, or else oftentimes of himself he fell into such deep thoughts of this enterprise, casting in his mind all the dangers that might happen, that his wife, lying by him, found that there was some marvellous great matter that troubled his mind, not being wont to be in that taking, and that he could not well determine with himself.

The glory of the theatre is that it can bring the interior character to life. In Act one, we see the public face of an apparently untroubled Brutus, but at the beginning of Act two Shakespeare conjures up the atmosphere of night, takes Brutus from his bed and places him alone of the bare boards of the Globe. The art of soliloquy then allows us to enter into that troubled mind, to weigh the greatness of the danger, to share the deep thoughts of the enterprise:

> It must be by his death: and for my part,
> I know no personal cause to spurn at him
> But for the general. He would be crowned:
> How that might change his nature, there's the question.

There's the question. Anton Chekhov, perhaps the greatest dramatist since Shakespeare, said that the business of the dramatist is not to provide solutions but to pose problems in the correct way. *Julius Caesar* doesn't give us easy answers about the relationship of public duty to private will. Shakespeare was content to dramatize the problem and leave the rest to his audience.

ABOUT THE TEXT

Shakespeare endures through history. He illuminates later times as well as his own. He helps us to understand the human condition. But he cannot do this without a good text of the plays. Without editions there would be no Shakespeare. That is why every twenty years or so throughout the last three centuries there has been a major new edition of his complete works. One aspect of editing is the process of keeping the texts up to date – modernizing the spelling, punctuation and typography (though not, of course, the actual words), providing explanatory notes in the light of changing educational practices (a generation ago, most of Shakespeare's classical and biblical allusions could be assumed to be generally understood, but now they can't).

Because Shakespeare did not personally oversee the publication of his plays, with some plays there are major editorial difficulties. Decisions have to be made as to the relative authority of the early printed editions, the pocket format 'Quartos' published in Shakespeare's lifetime and the elaborately produced 'First Folio' text of 1623, the original 'Complete Works' prepared for the press after his death by Shakespeare's fellow-actors, the people who knew the plays better than anyone else. *Julius Caesar*, however, exists only in a Folio text that is exceptionally well printed, showing every sign that the copy from which the compositors were working was legible and clear. The following notes highlight various aspects of the editorial process and indicate conventions used in the text of this edition:

Lists of Parts are supplied in the First Folio for only six plays, not including *Julius Caesar*, so the list here is editorially supplied. Capitals indicate that part of the name used for speech headings in the script (thus 'Marcus BRUTUS, sometime friend of Caesar, then conspirator against him').

Locations are provided by the Folio for only two plays, of which *Julius Caesar* is not one. Eighteenth-century editors, working in an age of elaborately realistic stage sets, were the first to provide detailed locations ('*another part of the city*'). Given that Shakespeare wrote for a bare stage and often an imprecise sense of place, we have relegated locations to the explanatory notes at the foot of the page, where they are given at the beginning of each scene where the imaginary location is different from the one before. In the case of *Julius Caesar* the action takes place in Rome apart from Brutus' camp near Sardis and the final battle at Philippi.

Act and Scene Divisions were provided in the Folio in a much more thoroughgoing way than in the Quartos. Sometimes, however, they were erroneous or omitted; corrections and additions supplied by editorial tradition are indicated by square brackets. Five-act division is based on a classical model, and act breaks provided the opportunity to replace the candles in the indoor Blackfriars playhouse which the King's Men used after 1608, but Shakespeare did not necessarily think in terms of a five-part structure of dramatic composition. The Folio convention is that a scene ends when the stage is empty. Nowadays, partly under the influence of film, we tend to consider a scene to be a dramatic unit that ends with either a change of imaginary location or a significant passage of time within the narrative. Shakespeare's fluidity of composition accords well with this convention, so in addition to act and scene numbers we provide a *running scene* count in the right margin at the beginning of each new scene, in the typeface used for editorial directions. Where there is a scene break caused by a momentary bare stage, but the location does not change and extra time does not pass, we use the convention *running scene continues*. There is inevitably a degree of editorial judgement in making such calls, but the system is very valuable in suggesting the pace of the plays.

Speakers' Names are often inconsistent in the Folio. We have regularized speech headings, but retained an element of deliberate inconsistency in entry directions, in order to give the flavour of Folio.

Verse is indicated by lines that do not run to the right margin and by capitalization of each line. The Folio printers sometimes set verse as prose, and vice versa (either out of misunderstanding or for reasons of space). We have silently corrected in such cases, although in some instances there is ambiguity, in which case we have leaned towards the preservation of Folio layout. Folio sometimes uses contraction ('turnd' rather than 'turned') to indicate whether or not the final '-ed' of a past participle is sounded, an area where there is variation for the sake of the five-beat iambic pentameter rhythm. We use the convention of a grave accent to indicate sounding (thus 'turnèd' would be two syllables), but would urge actors not to overstress. In cases where one speaker ends with a verse half-line and the next begins with the other half of the pentameter, editors since the late eighteenth century have indented the second line. We have abandoned this convention, since the Folio does not use it, and nor did actors' cues in the Shakespearean theatre. An exception is made when the second speaker actively interrupts or completes the first speaker's sentence.

Spelling is modernized, but older forms are very occasionally maintained where necessary for rhythm or aural effect.

Punctuation in Shakespeare's time was as much rhetorical as grammatical. 'Colon' was originally a term for a unit of thought in an argument. The semi-colon was a new unit of punctuation (some of the Quartos lack them altogether). We have modernized punctuation throughout, but have given more weight to Folio punctuation than many editors, since, though not Shakespearean, it reflects the usage of his period. In particular, we have used the colon far more than many editors: it is exceptionally useful as a way of indicating how many Shakespearean speeches unfold clause by clause in a developing argument that gives the illusion of enacting the process of thinking in the moment. We have also kept in mind the origin of punctuation in classical times as a way of assisting the actor and orator: the comma suggests the briefest of pauses for breath, the colon a middling one and a full stop or period a longer pause. Semi-colons, by contrast, belong to an era of punctuation that was only just coming in during Shakespeare's time and that is coming to an end now: we have accordingly only used them where they occur in our copy-texts (and not always then). Dashes are sometimes used for parenthetical interjections where the Folio has brackets. They are also used for interruptions and changes in train of thought. Where a change of addressee occurs within a speech, we have used a dash preceded by a full stop (or occasionally another form of punctuation). Often the identity of the respective addressees is obvious from the context. When it is not, this has been indicated in a marginal stage direction.

Entrances and Exits are fairly thorough in Folio, which has accordingly been followed as faithfully as possible. Where characters are omitted or corrections are necessary, this is indicated by square brackets (e.g. '[*and Attendants*]'). *Exit* is sometimes silently normalized to *Exeunt* and *Manet* anglicized to 'remains'. We trust Folio positioning of entrances and exits to a greater degree than most editors.

Editorial Stage Directions such as stage business, asides, indications of addressee and of characters' position on the gallery stage are only used sparingly in Folio. Other editions mingle directions of this kind with original Folio and Quarto directions, sometimes marking them by means of square brackets. We have sought to distinguish what could be described as *directorial* interventions of this kind from Folio-style directions (either original or supplied) by placing them in the right margin in a different typeface. There is a degree of subjectivity about which directions are of which kind, but the procedure is intended as a reminder to the reader and the actor that Shakespearean stage directions are often dependent upon editorial inference alone and are not set in stone. We also depart from editorial tradition in sometimes admitting uncertainty and thus printing permissive stage-directions, such as an *Aside?* (often a line may be equally effective as an aside or a direct address – it is for each production or reading to make its own decision) or a *may exit* or a piece of business placed between arrows to indicate that it may occur at various different moments within a scene.

Line Numbers in the left margin are editorial, for reference and to key the explanatory and textual notes.

Explanatory Notes at the foot of each page explain allusions and gloss obsolete and difficult words, confusing phraseology, occasional major textual cruces, and so on. Particular attention is given to non-standard usage, bawdy innuendo and technical terms (e.g. legal and military language). Where more than one sense is given, commas indicate shades of related meaning, slashes alternative or double meanings.

Textual Notes at the end of the play indicate major departures from the Folio. They take the following form: the reading of our text is given in bold and its source given after an equals sign, with 'F2' indicating a correction that derives from the Second Folio of 1632, 'F3' a correction introduced in the Third Folio of 1664, and 'Ed' one that derives from the subsequent editorial tradition. The rejected Folio ('F') reading is then given. Thus for Act 5 scene 4 line 18: '**tell the** = Ed. F = tell thee' means that the Folio text's 'tell thee' has been rejected in favour of the editorial correction 'tell the', which makes better sense of the rest of the First Soldier's speech.

KEY FACTS

MAJOR PARTS: (with percentage of lines/number of speeches/ scenes on stage) Marcus Brutus (28%/194/12), Caius Cassius (20%/ 140/8), Mark Antony (13%/51/8), Julius Caesar (5%/42/4), Casca (5%/39/4), Portia (4%/16/2), Octavius Caesar (2%/19/3), Decius Brutus (2%/12/3).

LINGUISTIC MEDIUM: 95% verse, 5% prose.

DATE: 1599. Not mentioned by Meres in 1598, seen at the Globe by Swiss visitor Thomas Platter in September 1599. Alluded to in several plays and poems by other writers in the period 1599–1601.

SOURCES: Based on the biographies of Julius Caesar and Marcus Brutus, with brief reference to the life of Cicero, in Sir Thomas North's English translation of Plutarch's *Lives of the Most Noble Grecians and Romanes* (1579).

TEXT: 1623 Folio is the only early printed text. Exceptionally good quality of printing, perhaps set from the theatre promptbook or a transcription of it. Some editors have detected signs of revision in the fact that Brutus is told twice of Portia's suicide, and proposed that one or other account should be deleted, but in the theatre this double testing of his Stoic response is highly effective.

THE TRAGEDY OF JULIUS CAESAR

Julius **CAESAR**

CALPURNIA, his wife

Marcus **BRUTUS**, sometime friend of Caesar, then conspirator against him

PORTIA, his wife

Caius **CASSIUS**

CASCA

DECIUS Brutus

CINNA

METELLUS Cimber

TREBONIUS

Caius **LIGARIUS**

⎱ other conspirators against Caesar

Mark **ANTONY**

OCTAVIUS Caesar

LEPIDUS

⎱ triumvirs of Rome after Caesar's death

A **SOOTHSAYER**

ARTEMIDORUS, a teacher of rhetoric

CINNA, a poet

Another **POET**

CICERO

PUBLIUS

POPILIUS

⎱ senators

MURELLUS

FLAVIUS

⎱ tribunes of the people

A **CARPENTER**

A **COBBLER**

FIRST, SECOND, THIRD, FOURTH and **FIFTH PLEBEIANS**

LUCIUS, Brutus' young servant

PINDARUS, Cassius' bondman

LUCILIUS

TITINIUS

MESSALA

CATO

STRATO

CLAUDIO

VARRUS

CLITUS

DARDANIUS

VOLUMNIUS

⎱ supporters of Brutus and Cassius

SERVANT, to Caesar

SERVANT, to Antony

SERVANT, to Octavius

A **MESSENGER**

FIRST, SECOND and **THIRD SOLDIERS**, members of Brutus and Cassius' army

FIRST and **SECOND SOLDIERS**, members of Antony's army

GHOST, Caesar's ghost

Other Commoners, Senators and Soldiers

Act 1 Scene 1

Enter Flavius, Murellus and certain Commoners over the
stage

FLAVIUS Hence! Home, you idle creatures, get you home:
Is this a holiday? What, know you not,
Being mechanical, you ought not walk
Upon a labouring day, without the sign
5   Of your profession?— Speak, what trade art thou?
CARPENTER Why, sir, a carpenter.
MURELLUS Where is thy leather apron, and thy rule?
What dost thou with thy best apparel on?—
You, sir, what trade are you?
10   **COBBLER** Truly, sir, in respect of a fine workman, I am
but as you would say, a cobbler.
MURELLUS But what trade art thou? Answer me directly.
COBBLER A trade, sir, that I hope, I may use with a safe
conscience, which is indeed, sir, a mender of bad
15   soles.
FLAVIUS What trade, thou knave? Thou naughty knave,
what trade?
COBBLER Nay I beseech you, sir, be not out with me: yet
if you be out, sir, I can mend you.
MURELLUS What mean'st thou by that? Mend me, thou
saucy fellow?
20   **COBBLER** Why sir, cobble you.
FLAVIUS Thou art a cobbler, art thou?
COBBLER Truly sir, all that I live by is with the awl. I
meddle with no tradesman's matters, nor women's
matters; but withal I am indeed, sir, a surgeon to
25   old shoes: when they are in great danger, I
recover them. As proper men as ever trod upon
neat's leather have gone upon my handiwork.

1.1 *Location: a public place in Rome* **1 Hence!** Get away! **3 mechanical** working men, artisans
walk be out and about **4 sign** i.e. clothing, tools **7 rule** measuring stick (plays on the sense of 'decorum,
discipline') **10 in respect of** compared with **fine workman** skilled craftsman **11 but** merely **cobbler**
shoe-mender/one who mends clumsily **12 directly** plainly/immediately **15 soles** puns on 'souls'
16 naughty wicked **17 be not out** do not be angry/do not have holes in your shoes **18 mend you** repair
your shoes/improve your temper **20 cobble** fix; plays on the sense of 'have sex with' **22 awl** shoe-
mending tool used to prick leather/penis **23 meddle** get involved/have sex **tradesman's matters**
professional issues/sex/prostitution **women's matters** the concerns of women/sex or perhaps 'vaginas'
24 withal nevertheless (puns on **with all/awl**) **25 shoes** plays on sense of 'vaginas' **26 recover** patch/
restore to health (may play on sense of 'cover with my body during sex') **proper** fine/handsome **trod**
upon plays on sense of 'had sex with' **neat's leather** cowhide, i.e. shoes; **leather** could also be slang for
'vagina' **27 gone upon** walked on/had sex with **handiwork** possible connotations of masturbation

FLAVIUS But wherefore art not in thy shop today?
Why dost thou lead these men about the streets?

30 **COBBLER** Truly, sir, to wear out their shoes, to get
myself into more work. But indeed, sir, we make
holiday to see Caesar and to rejoice in his triumph.

MURELLUS Wherefore rejoice? What conquest brings he
home?
What tributaries follow him to Rome

35 To grace in captive bonds his chariot wheels?
You blocks, you stones, you worse than senseless
things:
O you hard hearts, you cruel men of Rome,
Knew you not Pompey? Many a time and oft
Have you climbed up to walls and battlements,

40 To towers and windows? Yea, to chimney-tops,
Your infants in your arms, and there have sat
The livelong day, with patient expectation,
To see great Pompey pass the streets of Rome:
And when you saw his chariot but appear,

45 Have you not made an universal shout,
That Tiber trembled underneath her banks
To hear the replication of your sounds
Made in her concave shores?
And do you now put on your best attire?

50 And do you now cull out a holiday?
And do you now strew flowers in his way
That comes in triumph over Pompey's blood?
Be gone!
Run to your houses, fall upon your knees,

55 Pray to the gods to intermit the plague
That needs must light on this ingratitude.

FLAVIUS Go, go, good countrymen, and for this fault
Assemble all the poor men of your sort;
Draw them to Tiber banks, and weep your tears

60 Into the channel till the lowest stream
Do kiss the most exalted shores of all.—
                              Exeunt all the Commoners

---

28 **wherefore** why   32 **triumph** victory/ceremonious procession in which the victors rode in chariots with
their captives chained   34 **tributaries** prisoners of war (for whom a ransom would be demanded)
35 **grace** adorn   38 **Pompey** great Roman general defeated by Caesar at the battle of Pharsalus in 48 BC;
he fled to Egypt where he was murdered   42 **livelong** entire   46 **That** so that   **Tiber** Rome's river
47 **replication** reverberation, echo   48 **concave** hollowed out/curved   50 **cull out** choose for yourself
52 **blood** life-blood/relatives (specifically, his sons, who were also defeated by Caesar)   55 **intermit** stop
60 **till . . . all** i.e. until the water level rises from its very lowest to reach the highest banks

See where their basest mettle be not moved:
They vanish tongue-tied in their guiltiness.
Go you down that way towards the Capitol,
65   This way will I: disrobe the images
If you do find them decked with ceremonies.
MURELLUS May we do so?
You know it is the feast of Lupercal.
FLAVIUS It is no matter. Let no images
70   Be hung with Caesar's trophies. I'll about
And drive away the vulgar from the streets;
So do you too, where you perceive them thick.
These growing feathers plucked from Caesar's wing
Will make him fly an ordinary pitch,
75   Who else would soar above the view of men,
And keep us all in servile fearfulness.   *Exeunt*

[Act 1 Scene 2]   *running scene 1 continues*

*Enter Caesar, Antony for the course, Calpurnia, Portia,
Decius, Cicero, Brutus, Cassius, Casca, a Soothsayer, after
them Murellus and Flavius*

CAESAR Calpurnia.
CASCA Peace, ho! Caesar speaks.
CAESAR Calpurnia.
CALPURNIA Here, my lord.
5   **CAESAR** Stand you directly in Antonio's way
When he doth run his course. Antonio!
ANTONY Caesar, my lord.
CAESAR Forget not in your speed, Antonio,
To touch Calpurnia, for our elders say,
10   The barren touchèd in this holy chase
Shake off their sterile curse.

---

62 basest mettle lowly dispositions/base metal (an image from alchemy, the pseudo-science that sought to turn base metals into gold)   **moved** stirred, persuaded/changed (into gold)   **64 Capitol** Capitoline Hill, site of the temple of supreme Roman god Jupiter; used in the play as the location of the senate house
65 images statues of Caesar   **66 ceremonies** ornamental trappings of state/worshipful tokens   **68 feast of Lupercal** Roman festival held on 15 February in honour of Lupercus, the god of shepherds; festivities centred around the Lupercal, a cave in which a wolf was believed to have suckled Rome's founders, Romulus and Remus   **70 trophies** tokens of victory   **about** walk about (the city)   **71 vulgar** common people
72 thick numerous, thronging   **74 pitch** height (achieved by bird of prey before swooping)   **75 else** otherwise   **1.2** *for* ready for   *course* wearing nothing but goat-skins, youths celebrating the festival of Lupercal ran round Palatine Hill, striking women with strips of goat hide to promote fertility   *Soothsayer* prophet   **2 ho** a call for attention   **5 Stand ... course** in order that Calpurnia should be touched by Antony, as an aid to fertility

ANTONY I shall remember.

When Caesar says 'Do this' it is performed.

CAESAR Set on, and leave no ceremony out.   *Music*

15 SOOTHSAYER Caesar!

CAESAR Ha? Who calls?

CASCA Bid every noise be still: peace yet again!   *Music stops*

CAESAR Who is it in the press that calls on me?

I hear a tongue shriller than all the music,

20   Cry 'Caesar!' Speak, Caesar is turned to hear.

SOOTHSAYER Beware the Ides of March.

CAESAR What man is that?

BRUTUS A soothsayer bids you beware the Ides of March.

CAESAR Set him before me: let me see his face.

25 CASSIUS Fellow, come from the throng: look upon
        Caesar.   *Soothsayer comes forward*

CAESAR What say'st thou to me now? Speak once again.

SOOTHSAYER Beware the Ides of March.

CAESAR He is a dreamer. Let us leave him: pass.

        Sennet.   Exeunt. Brutus and Cassius remain

CASSIUS Will you go see the order of the course?

30 BRUTUS Not I.

CASSIUS I pray you do.

BRUTUS I am not gamesome: I do lack some part

Of that quick spirit that is in Antony.

Let me not hinder, Cassius, your desires;

35   I'll leave you.

CASSIUS Brutus, I do observe you now of late:

I have not from your eyes that gentleness

And show of love as I was wont to have:

You bear too stubborn and too strange a hand

40   Over your friend, that loves you.

BRUTUS Cassius,

Be not deceived: if I have veiled my look,

I turn the trouble of my countenance

Merely upon myself. Vexed I am

45   Of late with passions of some difference,

Conceptions only proper to myself

Which give some soil, perhaps, to my behaviours.

---

18 press crowd   **21 Ides of March** 15 March   **28 *Sennet*** trumpet call signalling a procession   **29 order** arrangement/proceedings   **32 gamesome** fond of sport/lively/merry   **33 quick** lively   **36 now of late** lately   **38 wont** accustomed   **39 bear...Over** are too unyielding and unfamiliar towards

42 if...myself i.e. if I have seemed distant, it is because I have directed all my anxieties inward   **44 Merely** entirely   **45 passions...difference** conflicting emotions/powerful feelings that have come between myself and my friends   **46 Conceptions** thoughts   **only proper** belonging only/only appropriate   **47 soil** stain/explanation

But let not therefore my good friends be grieved —
Among which number, Cassius, be you one —
50 Nor construe any further my neglect
Than that poor Brutus, with himself at war,
Forgets the shows of love to other men.

CASSIUS Then, Brutus, I have much mistook your
    passion,
By means whereof this breast of mine hath buried
55 Thoughts of great value, worthy cogitations.
Tell me, good Brutus, can you see your face?

BRUTUS No, Cassius, for the eye sees not itself
But by reflection, by some other things.

CASSIUS 'Tis just,
60 And it is very much lamented, Brutus,
That you have no such mirrors as will turn
Your hidden worthiness into your eye,
That you might see your shadow: I have heard,
Where many of the best respect in Rome —
65 Except immortal Caesar — speaking of Brutus,
And groaning underneath this age's yoke,
Have wished that noble Brutus had his eyes.

BRUTUS Into what dangers would you lead me, Cassius,
That you would have me seek into myself
70 For that which is not in me?

CASSIUS Therefore, good Brutus, be prepared to hear:
And since you know you cannot see yourself
So well as by reflection, I your glass
Will modestly discover to yourself
75 That of yourself which you yet know not of.
And be not jealous on me, gentle Brutus:
Were I a common laughter, or did use
To stale with ordinary oaths my love
To every new protester, if you know
80 That I do fawn on men, and hug them hard,
And after scandal them, or if you know

---

50 construe interpret, understand   **52 shows** outward manifestations   **54 By means whereof** as a result of which **buried** kept to itself/suppressed/put to rest   **55 cogitations** thoughts, ideas   **58 But** except   **59 just** true   **61 turn** return/reflect   **63 shadow** reflection   **64 of . . . respect** most highly regarded men   **66 yoke** apparatus worn on the neck, used to restrict the movement of a captive or conquered enemy   **67 had his eyes** i.e. saw things for himself/saw things as the speaker did   **71 Therefore** hence/as for that   **73 glass** mirror   **74 modestly** without exaggeration   **discover** reveal   **75 That . . . of** i.e. your potential   **76 jealous on** mistrustful of   **gentle** noble/kind   **77 common laughter** subject of public ridicule   **did use** were I accustomed   **78 stale** make stale/depreciate/make into a laughing-stock **ordinary** common, banal   **79 protester** declarer of friendship   **81 scandal** scorn/slander

That I profess myself in banqueting
To all the rout, then hold me dangerous.

Flourish, and shout

BRUTUS What means this shouting? I do fear the people
85   Choose Caesar for their king.

CASSIUS Ay, do you fear it?
Then must I think you would not have it so.

BRUTUS I would not, Cassius, yet I love him well.
But wherefore do you hold me here so long?
90   What is it that you would impart to me?
If it be aught toward the general good,
Set honour in one eye, and death i'th'other,
And I will look on both indifferently.
For let the gods so speed me, as I love
95   The name of honour more than I fear death.

CASSIUS I know that virtue to be in you, Brutus,
As well as I do know your outward favour.
Well, honour is the subject of my story:
I cannot tell what you and other men
100   Think of this life, but for my single self,
I had as lief not be as live to be
In awe of such a thing as I myself.
I was born free as Caesar, so were you:
We both have fed as well, and we can both
105   Endure the winter's cold as well as he,
For once, upon a raw and gusty day,
The troubled Tiber chafing with her shores,
Caesar said to me, 'Dar'st thou, Cassius, now
Leap in with me into this angry flood
110   And swim to yonder point?' Upon the word,
Accoutrèd as I was, I plungèd in
And bade him follow: so indeed he did.
The torrent roared, and we did buffet it
With lusty sinews, throwing it aside,
115   And stemming it with hearts of controversy.
But ere we could arrive the point proposed,
Caesar cried, 'Help me, Cassius, or I sink!'

---

82 profess myself declare friendship   **83 rout** rabble/assembled company   **83 *Flourish*** trumpet fanfare accompanying a person in authority   **91 aught** anything   **92 Set . . . i'th'other** i.e. present me with both **93 indifferently** impartially   **94 speed** prosper   **97 favour** appearance/face   **101 as lief** as soon, rather be exist   **102 such . . . myself** i.e. a fellow man   **107 chafing with** fretting at/raging against   **109 flood** river   **111 Accoutrèd** dressed   **112 bade** invited/told   **113 buffet it** beat it back   **114 lusty sinews** vigorous muscles, strong arms   **115 stemming** cutting through   **hearts of controversy** competitive hearts, contentious spirits   **116 ere** before

I — as Aeneas, our great ancestor,
Did from the flames of Troy upon his shoulder
120 The old Anchises bear — so from the waves of Tiber
Did I the tired Caesar: and this man
Is now become a god, and Cassius is
A wretched creature, and must bend his body
If Caesar carelessly but nod on him.
125 He had a fever when he was in Spain,
And when the fit was on him I did mark
How he did shake: 'tis true, this god did shake,
His coward lips did from their colour fly,
And that same eye, whose bend doth awe the world,
130 Did lose his lustre: I did hear him groan:
Ay, and that tongue of his that bade the Romans
Mark him, and write his speeches in their books,
'Alas', it cried, 'Give me some drink, Titinius',
As a sick girl. Ye gods, it doth amaze me
135 A man of such a feeble temper should
So get the start of the majestic world
And bear the palm alone.
Shout. Flourish
BRUTUS Another general shout?
I do believe that these applauses are
140 For some new honours that are heaped on Caesar.
CASSIUS Why, man, he doth bestride the narrow world
Like a Colossus, and we petty men
Walk under his huge legs and peep about
To find ourselves dishonourable graves.
145 Men at some time are masters of their fates.
The fault, dear Brutus, is not in our stars
But in ourselves, that we are underlings.
Brutus and Caesar: what should be in that 'Caesar'?
Why should that name be sounded more than yours?
150 Write them together, yours is as fair a name:
Sound them, it doth become the mouth as well:
Weigh them, it is as heavy: conjure with 'em,
Brutus will start a spirit as soon as Caesar.

---

118 Aeneas legendary founder of Rome; Virgil's *Aeneid* relates how he carried his old father, **Anchises**, on his back as they escaped from the burning city of Troy   **123 bend his body** i.e. bow   **126 mark** note, observe   **128 from...fly** i.e. became pale (**colour** plays on the sense of 'military flag', the **lips** being cowardly deserters)   **129 bend** gaze   **131 bade** ordered   **136 start of** advantage over   **137 palm** palm leaf, symbol of victory   **142 Colossus** giant; the Colossus of Rhodes, a gigantic statue of the sun god Apollo, supposedly stood astride the entrance to the harbour   **145 at some time** at times   **146 our stars** i.e. fate   **149 be sounded** be spoken/resound/be celebrated   **152 conjure** invoke spirits   **153 start** raise, awake

Now in the names of all the gods at once,
155 Upon what meat doth this our Caesar feed
That he is grown so great? — Age, thou art
    shamed! —
Rome, thou hast lost the breed of noble bloods! —
When went there by an age, since the great flood,
But it was famed with more than with one man?
160 When could they say, till now, that talked of Rome,
That her wide walks encompassed but one man?
Now is it Rome indeed, and room enough
When there is in it but one only man.
O, you and I have heard our fathers say
165 There was a Brutus once that would have brooked
Th'eternal devil to keep his state in Rome
As easily as a king.

BRUTUS That you do love me, I am nothing jealous:
What you would work me to, I have some aim:
170 How I have thought of this and of these times
I shall recount hereafter. For this present,
I would not — so with love I might entreat you —
Be any further moved. What you have said
I will consider, what you have to say
175 I will with patience hear, and find a time
Both meet to hear and answer such high things.
Till then, my noble friend, chew upon this:
Brutus had rather be a villager
Than to repute himself a son of Rome
180 Under these hard conditions as this time
Is like to lay upon us.

CASSIUS I am glad that my weak words
Have struck but thus much show of fire from Brutus.
Enter Caesar and his train

BRUTUS The games are done, and Caesar is returning.
185 **CASSIUS** As they pass by, pluck Casca by the sleeve,
And he will, after his sour fashion, tell you
What hath proceeded worthy note today.

---

155 meat food   **156 great** powerful (plays on the sense of 'fat')   **Age** i.e. the present time   **157 breed of** ability to produce/supply of   **158 the great flood** feature of both the Bible and Greek mythology; in the classical flood, Zeus drowns all mankind except for Deucalion and his wife Pyrrha   **162 room** puns on **Rome** (the words were pronounced in a similar way)   **165 a Brutus once** i.e. Lucius Junius Brutus, who expelled the last King of Rome and founded the Roman republic   **brooked** tolerated, endured   **166 state** throne/ kingship   **168 nothing jealous** in no doubt   **169 work** persuade   **aim** idea, understanding   **172 so . . . you** if I may entreat you in friendship   **173 moved** urged, persuaded   **176 meet** fitting   **high** important   **179 repute** consider   **181 like** likely   **183 train** retinue   **186 after** according to   **187 worthy** that is worthy of

BRUTUS I will do so: but look you, Cassius,
The angry spot doth glow on Caesar's brow,
190   And all the rest look like a chidden train:
Calpurnia's cheek is pale, and Cicero
Looks with such ferret and such fiery eyes
As we have seen him in the Capitol
Being crossed in conference by some senators.
195   **CASSIUS** Casca will tell us what the matter is.
CAESAR Antonio.
ANTONY Caesar?
CAESAR Let me have men about me that are fat,
Sleek-headed men, and such as sleep a-nights.
200   Yond Cassius has a lean and hungry look:
He thinks too much: such men are dangerous.
ANTONY Fear him not, Caesar, he's not dangerous.
He is a noble Roman, and well given.
CAESAR Would he were fatter! But I fear him not:
205   Yet if my name were liable to fear,
I do not know the man I should avoid
So soon as that spare Cassius. He reads much,
He is a great observer, and he looks
Quite through the deeds of men. He loves no plays,
210   As thou dost, Antony: he hears no music:
Seldom he smiles, and smiles in such a sort
As if he mocked himself, and scorned his spirit
That could be moved to smile at anything.
Such men as he be never at heart's ease
215   Whiles they behold a greater than themselves,
And therefore are they very dangerous.
I rather tell thee what is to be feared
Than what I fear, for always I am Caesar.
Come on my right hand, for this ear is deaf,
220   And tell me truly what thou think'st of him.
                    Sennet.   Exeunt Caesar and his train
CASCA You pulled me by the cloak: would you speak
with me?
BRUTUS Ay, Casca, tell us what hath chanced today
That Caesar looks so sad.
225   **CASCA** Why, you were with him, were you not?

---

190 chidden scolded, rebuked   **192 ferret** ferret-like, i.e. small and red   **194 crossed** challenged
conference debate   **199 Sleek-headed** well-groomed, smooth-haired   **200 yond** i.e. yonder, over
there   **203 given** disposed   **204 Would** I wish   **205 my name** i.e. I   **207 spare** lean, gaunt   **208 looks**
...**deeds** i.e. sees right through to the motives behind men's actions   **211 sort** way   **215 greater** i.e.
greater man   **218 Caesar** i.e. not **liable to fear**   **223 chanced** happened   **224 sad** serious/downcast

BRUTUS I should not then ask Casca what had chanced.

CASCA Why, there was a crown offered him; and being
offered him, he put it by with the back of his hand,
thus, and then the people fell a-shouting.

230 **BRUTUS** What was the second noise for?

CASCA Why, for that too.

CASSIUS They shouted thrice: what was the last cry for?

CASCA Why, for that too.

BRUTUS Was the crown offered him thrice?

235 **CASCA** Ay, marry, was't, and he put it by thrice, every
time gentler than other; and at every putting-by,
mine honest neighbours shouted.

CASSIUS Who offered him the crown?

CASCA Why, Antony.

240 **BRUTUS** Tell us the manner of it, gentle Casca.

CASCA I can as well be hanged as tell the manner of it: it
was mere foolery, I did not mark it. I saw Mark
Antony offer him a crown — yet 'twas not a crown
neither, 'twas one of these coronets — and as I told
245 you, he put it by once: but for all that, to my
thinking, he would fain have had it. Then he offered
it to him again, then he put it by again: but to my
thinking, he was very loath to lay his fingers off it.
And then he offered it the third time; he put it the
250 third time by, and still as he refused it, the
rabblement hooted, and clapped their chopped
hands, and threw up their sweaty nightcaps, and
uttered such a deal of stinking breath because Caesar
refused the crown that it had almost choked Caesar,
255 for he swooned and fell down at it. And for mine own
part, I durst not laugh, for fear of opening my lips and
receiving the bad air.

CASSIUS But soft, I pray you: what, did Caesar swoon?

CASCA He fell down in the market-place, and foamed at
260 mouth, and was speechless.

BRUTUS 'Tis very like — he hath the falling sickness.

CASSIUS No, Caesar hath it not: but you, and I,
And honest Casca, we have the falling sickness.

---

227 crown laurel crown, symbol of kingship   **228 put it by** waved it away, declined it   **235 marry** indeed
(literally, 'by the Virgin Mary')   **236 gentler** more courteously/with less insistence   **242 mere**
complete   **244 coronets** smaller crowns, inferior to that worn by a king   **246 fain** willingly   **250 still as**
whenever   **251 rabblement** crowd, rabble   **chopped** chapped, roughened   **252 nightcaps** a slighting
reference to their headgear, not to caps worn in bed   **256 durst** dared   **258 soft** wait a moment   **261 like**
likely   **the falling sickness** epilepsy   **263 we . . . sickness** i.e. our fortunes are falling, we are neglected

CASCA I know not what you mean by that, but I am sure
265   Caesar fell down. If the tag-rag people did not clap
        him and hiss him according as he pleased and
        displeased them, as they use to do the players in the
        theatre, I am no true man.

BRUTUS What said he when he came unto himself?

270 CASCA Marry, before he fell down, when he perceived
        the common herd was glad he refused the crown,
        he plucked me ope his doublet and offered them his
        throat to cut: an I had been a man of any
        occupation, if I would not have taken him at a
275   word, I would I might go to hell among the rogues.
        And so he fell. When he came to himself again, he
        said if he had done or said anything amiss, he
        desired their worships to think it was his infirmity.
        Three or four wenches where I stood cried 'Alas,
280   good soul!' and forgave him with all their hearts:
        but there's no heed to be taken of them; if Caesar
        had stabbed their mothers, they would have done
        no less.

BRUTUS And after that he came thus sad away.

285 CASCA Ay.

CASSIUS Did Cicero say anything?

CASCA Ay, he spoke Greek.

CASSIUS To what effect?

CASCA Nay, and I tell you that, I'll ne'er look you
290   i'th'face again. But those that understood him
        smiled at one another, and shook their heads: but,
        for mine own part, it was Greek to me. I could tell
        you more news too: Murellus and Flavius, for
        pulling scarves off Caesar's images, are put to
295   silence. Fare you well. There was more foolery yet,
        if I could remember it.

CASSIUS Will you sup with me tonight, Casca?

CASCA No, I am promised forth.

CASSIUS Will you dine with me tomorrow?

300 CASCA Ay, if I be alive, and your mind hold, and your
        dinner worth the eating.

---

265 **tag-rag** ragged   267 **use** are accustomed   268 **true** honest   272 **plucked me** plucked (**me** is an intensifier)   **ope** open   **doublet** close-fitting Elizabethan man's jacket   273 **an** if   **a … occupation** i.e. a working man, one of the crowd (plays on sense of 'a man of action')   274 **taken … word** taken him at his word (**taken** plays on sense of 'struck')   275 **would** wish   282 **stabbed** plays on sense of 'penetrated sexually'   292 **Greek to me** i.e. unintelligible   294 **put to silence** i.e. removed from office (or possibly 'put to death')   298 **promised forth** engaged to dine elsewhere   300 **mind hold** inclination doesn't change

CASSIUS Good, I will expect you.

CASCA Do so. Farewell, both.   *Exit*

BRUTUS What a blunt fellow is this grown to be!
305   He was quick mettle when he went to school.

CASSIUS So is he now, in execution
         Of any bold or noble enterprise,
         However he puts on this tardy form.
         This rudeness is a sauce to his good wit,
310   Which gives men stomach to digest his words
         With better appetite.

BRUTUS And so it is. For this time I will leave you:
         Tomorrow if you please to speak with me,
         I will come home to you: or if you will,
315   Come home to me, and I will wait for you.

CASSIUS I will do so. Till then, think of the world.
                                          Exit Brutus

         Well, Brutus, thou art noble: yet I see
         Thy honourable mettle may be wrought
         From that it is disposed: therefore it is meet
320   That noble minds keep ever with their likes
         For who so firm that cannot be seduced?
         Caesar doth bear me hard, but he loves Brutus.
         If I were Brutus now, and he were Cassius,
         He should not humour me. I will this night
325   In several hands in at his windows throw,
         As if they came from several citizens,
         Writings all tending to the great opinion
         That Rome holds of his name — wherein obscurely
         Caesar's ambition shall be glanced at.
330   And after this let Caesar seat him sure,
         For we will shake him, or worse days endure.   *Exit*

---

304 blunt forthright/dull   **305 quick mettle** lively spirited, quick-witted   **308 tardy** sluggish, reluctant
309 rudeness rough, uncouth manner   **wit** intelligence   **310 stomach** appetite, inclination   **314 home**
to you to your house   **316 the world** i.e. the state of Rome/your civic duty   **317 noble** begins an
alchemical metaphor: 'noble' metals (gold and silver) cannot be transmuted into base substances (though
despite this, Cassius thinks he can alter Brutus)   **318 mettle** spirit, disposition (puns on 'metal')   **wrought**
manipulated/transmuted   **319 that . . . disposed** its usual inclination/its natural disposition   **meet** right,
fitting   **320 their likes** those like them   **321 who** i.e. who is   **322 bear me hard** tolerate me grudgingly,
dislike me   **324 He . . . me** i.e. Brutus would not be able to sway my views (as I do his)/Caesar would still not
be able to entice me   **325 several hands** different styles of handwriting   **327 tending to** concerning
328 obscurely covertly, subtly   **329 glanced** hinted   **330 seat him sure** seat himself most securely (in
the chair of power), i.e. 'take great care'

[Act 1 Scene 3]

Thunder and lightning. Enter Casca and Cicero

CICERO Good even, Casca. Brought you Caesar home?
Why are you breathless, and why stare you so?
CASCA Are not you moved, when all the sway of earth
Shakes like a thing unfirm? O Cicero,
5   I have seen tempests, when the scolding winds
Have rived the knotty oaks, and I have seen
Th'ambitious ocean swell, and rage, and foam,
To be exalted with the threatening clouds:
But never till tonight, never till now,
10   Did I go through a tempest dropping fire.
Either there is a civil strife in heaven,
Or else the world, too saucy with the gods,
Incenses them to send destruction.
CICERO Why, saw you anything more wonderful?
15   **CASCA** A common slave — you know him well by
sight —
Held up his left hand, which did flame and burn
Like twenty torches joined; and yet his hand,
Not sensible of fire, remained unscorched.
Besides — I ha' not since put up my sword —
20   Against the Capitol I met a lion,
Who glazed upon me and went surly by
Without annoying me. And there were drawn
Upon a heap a hundred ghastly women,
Transformèd with their fear, who swore they saw
25   Men, all in fire, walk up and down the streets.
And yesterday the bird of night did sit
Even at noonday upon the market-place
Hooting and shrieking. When these prodigies
Do so conjointly meet, let not men say
30   'These are their reasons, they are natural',
For I believe they are portentous things
Unto the climate that they point upon.

1.3   1 even evening   **Brought** accompanied   **3 moved** upset, affected   **sway** order, rule, authority
(plays on sense of 'swinging movement')   **5 scolding** clamouring/rebuking   **6 rived** split   **8 exalted with**
raised up to   **12 saucy** insolent, defiant   **14 wonderful** astonishing, extraordinary   **18 sensible of**
feeling   **19 put up** sheathed   **20 Against** close to/in front of   **21 glazed** stared   **22 annoying**
harming   **23 Upon** into   **heap** crowd   **ghastly** terrified   **26 bird of night** the owl, considered a bird of ill
omen; its cry was thought to herald death   **28 prodigies** unnatural things/bad omens   **29 conjointly**
meet happen in unison, coincide   **32 climate** region   **point upon** are directed at, happen in

CICERO Indeed, it is a strange-disposèd time:
But men may construe things after their fashion
35   Clean from the purpose of the things themselves.
Comes Caesar to the Capitol tomorrow?
CASCA He doth, for he did bid Antonio
Send word to you he would be there tomorrow.
CICERO Goodnight then, Casca: this disturbèd sky
40   Is not to walk in.
CASCA Farewell, Cicero.   *Exit Cicero*
Enter Cassius
CASSIUS Who's there?
CASCA A Roman.
CASSIUS Casca, by your voice.
45   **CASCA** Your ear is good. Cassius, what night is this?
CASSIUS A very pleasing night to honest men.
CASCA Whoever knew the heavens menace so?
CASSIUS Those that have known the earth so full of
        faults.
For my part, I have walked about the streets,
50   Submitting me unto the perilous night,
And thus unbracèd, Casca, as you see,
Have bared my bosom to the thunder-stone:
And when the cross blue lightning seemed to open
The breast of heaven, I did present myself
55   Even in the aim and very flash of it.
CASCA But wherefore did you so much tempt the
        heavens?
It is the part of men to fear and tremble
When the most mighty gods by tokens send
Such dreadful heralds to astonish us.
60   **CASSIUS** You are dull, Casca, and those sparks of life
That should be in a Roman you do want,
Or else you use not. You look pale, and gaze,
And put on fear, and cast yourself in wonder
To see the strange impatience of the heavens:
65   But if you would consider the true cause
Why all these fires, why all these gliding ghosts,
Why birds and beasts, from quality and kind,
Why old men, fools, and children calculate,

---

34 after their fashion in their own way   **35 Clean** utterly   **45 what** what kind of   **51 unbracèd** with doublet unbuttoned   **52 thunder-stone** thunderbolt   **53 cross** forked/hostile   **58 tokens** signs, omens   **59 dreadful** inspiring dread and fear   **heralds** messengers   **61 want** lack   **62 use not** ignore them   **64 impatience** anger   **67 from . . . kind** against their natures   **68 calculate** (are able to) interpret events

Why all these things change from their ordinance
70   Their natures and preformèd faculties
To monstrous quality, why, you shall find
That heaven hath infused them with these spirits
To make them instruments of fear and warning
Unto some monstrous state.
75   Now could I, Casca, name to thee a man
Most like this dreadful night
That thunders, lightens, opens graves and roars
As doth the lion in the Capitol:
A man no mightier than thyself, or me,
80   In personal action, yet prodigious grown
And fearful, as these strange eruptions are.
  CASCA 'Tis Caesar that you mean, is it not, Cassius?
  CASSIUS Let it be who it is, for Romans now
Have thews and limbs like to their ancestors;
85   But woe the while, our fathers' minds are dead,
And we are governed with our mothers' spirits:
Our yoke and sufferance show us womanish.
  CASCA Indeed, they say the senators tomorrow
Mean to establish Caesar as a king,
90   And he shall wear his crown by sea and land,
In every place, save here in Italy.
  CASSIUS I know where I will wear this dagger then:
Cassius from bondage will deliver Cassius.—
Therein, ye gods, you make the weak most strong;
95   Therein, ye gods, you tyrants do defeat.—
Nor stony tower, nor walls of beaten brass,
Nor airless dungeon, nor strong links of iron,
Can be retentive to the strength of spirit:
But life being weary of these worldly bars
100   Never lacks power to dismiss itself.
If I know this, know all the world besides,
That part of tyranny that I do bear
I can shake off at pleasure.   *Thunder still*
  CASCA So can I:
105   So every bondman in his own hand bears
The power to cancel his captivity.

---

69 ordinance appointed function   **70 preformèd** established, innate   **71 monstrous** unnatural
74 state condition, state of affairs/commonwealth (i.e. Rome)   **77 lightens** flashes lightning
80 prodigious ominous/unnatural   **81 fearful** frightening   **eruptions** disturbances   **84 thews** sinews,
muscles   **85 fathers** (noble) forefathers, ancestors   **87 yoke and sufferance** patience in servitude
90 by . . . land i.e. in all dominions   **93 from . . . Cassius** i.e. will commit suicide   **94 Therein** i.e. through
suicide   **98 be retentive to** confine, restrict   **99 bars** prison bars/obstacles   **101 know . . . besides** let it
be known by all the world   **102 bear** endure   **103 pleasure** will   **105 bondman** slave

CASSIUS And why should Caesar be a tyrant then?
  Poor man, I know he would not be a wolf,
  But that he sees the Romans are but sheep:
110 He were no lion, were not Romans hinds.
  Those that with haste will make a mighty fire
  Begin it with weak straws. What trash is Rome?
  What rubbish, and what offal, when it serves
  For the base matter to illuminate
115 So vile a thing as Caesar?— But, O grief,
  Where hast thou led me? I, perhaps, speak this
  Before a willing bondman: then I know
  My answer must be made. But I am armed,
  And dangers are to me indifferent.
120 CASCA You speak to Casca, and to such a man
  That is no fleering tell-tale. Hold, my hand:
  Be factious for redress of all these griefs
  And I will set this foot of mine as far
  As who goes farthest.   *They shake hands*
125 CASSIUS There's a bargain made.
  Now know you, Casca, I have moved already
  Some certain of the noblest-minded Romans
  To undergo with me an enterprise
  Of honourable dangerous consequence;
130 And I do know by this, they stay for me
  In Pompey's porch, for now this fearful night
  There is no stir or walking in the streets;
  And the complexion of the element
  In favour's like the work we have in hand,
135 Most bloody, fiery and most terrible.
  Enter Cinna
  CASCA Stand close awhile, for here comes one in haste.
  CASSIUS 'Tis Cinna, I do know him by his gait.
  He is a friend.— Cinna, where haste you so?
  CINNA To find out you. Who's that? Metellus Cimber?
140 CASSIUS No, it is Casca, one incorporate
  To our attempts. Am I not stayed for, Cinna?

---

110 hinds female deer/servants **111 make . . . fire** i.e. achieve fame, power **112 weak straws** i.e. the Roman people **trash** twigs, hedge-cuttings (i.e. paltry but flammable) **113 rubbish** debris from decayed buildings **offal** rubbish/wood shavings **115 vile** base, corrupt **118 My . . . made** I must answer for it (i.e. be punished/fight you) **121 fleering** sneering **Hold, my** enough, take my **122 factious** prepared to form a faction **123 set . . . mine** i.e. commit myself, proceed **124 who** whoever **130 this** this time, now **stay** wait **131 Pompey's porch** colonnade built by Pompey in 55 BC to provide shelter for spectators attending the Theatrum Pompei (**Pompey's theatre**) that was constructed at the same time **133 complexion** appearance/disposition **element** sky, heavens **134 favour** appearance/face **136 close** concealed **140 incorporate To** united to, part of **141 stayed** waited

CINNA I am glad on't. What a fearful night is this?
     There's two or three of us have seen strange
        sights.
CASSIUS Am I not stayed for? Tell me.
145 CINNA Yes, you are.
     O Cassius, if you could
     But win the noble Brutus to our party—
CASSIUS Be you content. Good Cinna, take this paper   *Gives paper*
     And look you lay it in the praetor's chair
150 Where Brutus may but find it. And throw this
     In at his window; set this up with wax
     Upon old Brutus' statue. All this done,
     Repair to Pompey's porch, where you shall find us.
     Is Decius Brutus and Trebonius there?
155 CINNA All but Metellus Cimber, and he's gone
     To seek you at your house. Well, I will hie,
     And so bestow these papers as you bade me.
CASSIUS That done, repair to Pompey's theatre.—

                                    Exit Cinna

     Come, Casca, you and I will yet ere day
160 See Brutus at his house: three parts of him
     Is ours already, and the man entire
     Upon the next encounter yields him ours.
CASCA O, he sits high in all the people's hearts:
     And that which would appear offence in us,
165 His countenance, like richest alchemy,
     Will change to virtue and to worthiness.
CASSIUS Him, and his worth, and our great need of
        him
     You have right well conceited. Let us go,
     For it is after midnight, and ere day
170 We will awake him and be sure of him.   *Exeunt*

[Act 2 Scene 1]
                                    running scene 2

Enter Brutus in his orchard

BRUTUS What, Lucius, ho?—   *Calls*
     I cannot by the progress of the stars
     Give guess how near to day.— Lucius, I say!—

142 on't of it 149 praetor high-ranking magistrate, i.e. Brutus 150 may...it i.e. cannot avoid finding it 151 set this up attach this 153 Repair make your way 156 hie hurry 165 countenance approval/face, appearance alchemy pseudo-science that sought to turn base metals into gold 168 conceited conceived of, understood/expressed with an elaborate image 2.1 Location: Brutus' garden, Rome orchard garden

I would it were my fault to sleep so soundly.—

5   When, Lucius, when? Awake, I say: what, Lucius!

Enter Lucius

LUCIUS Called you, my lord?

BRUTUS Get me a taper in my study, Lucius,

When it is lighted, come and call me here.

LUCIUS I will, my lord.   *Exit*

10 **BRUTUS** It must be by his death: and for my part,

I know no personal cause to spurn at him

But for the general. He would be crowned:

How that might change his nature, there's the
    question.

It is the bright day that brings forth the adder,

15 And that craves wary walking: crown him that,

And then I grant we put a sting in him,

That at his will he may do danger with.

Th'abuse of greatness is when it disjoins

Remorse from power: and to speak truth of Caesar,

20 I have not known when his affections swayed

More than his reason. But 'tis a common proof

That lowliness is young ambition's ladder

Whereto the climber upward turns his face.

But when he once attains the upmost round,

25 He then unto the ladder turns his back,

Looks in the clouds, scorning the base degrees

By which he did ascend: so Caesar may;

Then, lest he may, prevent. And since the quarrel

Will bear no colour for the thing he is,

30 Fashion it thus: that what he is, augmented,

Would run to these and these extremities:

And therefore think him as a serpent's egg

Which hatched, would as his kind grow mischievous,

And kill him in the shell.

Enter Lucius

35 **LUCIUS** The taper burneth in your closet, sir.

Searching the window for a flint, I found

---

5 **When** exclamation of impatience   7 **taper** candle   10 **his** i.e. Caesar's; Brutus is in mid-thought
11 **spurn** strike, kick   12 **general** general cause, public good   15 **craves** requires   **crown him that** i.e.
crown him   19 **Remorse** pity, compassion   20 **affections** emotions   **swayed** influenced, ruled (him)
21 **proof** experience   22 **lowliness** humility/pretended humbleness   **ladder** i.e. means of rising to power
24 **upmost round** highest rung   26 **base degrees** lower rungs/those of lower social status   28 **the . . . is**
our cause for complaint cannot be justified on the grounds of his current behaviour   **colour** good reason/
pretext   30 **Fashion** contrive/fabricate, pervert   **augmented** i.e. once he has been given more power
33 **as his kind** like the rest of its species   **mischievous** harmful, dangerous   35 **closet** private room

This paper, thus sealed up, and I am sure
It did not lie there when I went to bed.
Gives him the letter
BRUTUS Get you to bed again, it is not day.
40   Is not tomorrow, boy, the first of March?
LUCIUS I know not, sir.
BRUTUS Look in the calendar, and bring me word.
LUCIUS I will, sir.   *Exit*
BRUTUS The exhalations whizzing in the air
45   Give so much light that I may read by them.
Opens the letter and reads
        'Brutus thou sleep'st. Awake, and see thyself.
        Shall Rome, etc. Speak, strike, redress.' —
        'Brutus, thou sleep'st. Awake!'
        Such instigations have been often dropped
50   Where I have took them up.
        'Shall Rome, etc.' Thus must I piece it out:
        Shall Rome stand under one man's awe? What
            Rome?
        My ancestors did from the streets of Rome
        The Tarquin drive when he was called a king.
55   'Speak, strike, redress.' Am I entreated
        To speak and strike? O Rome, I make thee promise,
        If the redress will follow, thou receivest
        Thy full petition at the hand of Brutus.
Enter Lucius
LUCIUS Sir, March is wasted fifteen days.
Knock within
60 **BRUTUS** 'Tis good. Go to the gate: somebody knocks.—
                                        [*Exit Lucius*]
        Since Cassius first did whet me against Caesar,
        I have not slept.
        Between the acting of a dreadful thing
        And the first motion, all the interim is
65   Like a phantasma, or a hideous dream:
        The genius and the mortal instruments
        Are then in council, and the state of man,

---

44 **exhalations** meteors (considered bad omens, these were thought to consist of noxious vapours that had been drawn up, or 'exhaled', from the earth by the sun)   51 **piece it out** add to it, fill it out   54 **Tarquin** Tarquinius Superbus, the last King of Rome, who was expelled by Lucius Junius Brutus   58 **petition** request   61 **whet** incite (literally refers to sharpening of a knife)   64 **motion** suggestion/impulse   65 **phantasma** illusion, hallucination   66 **genius** attendant guardian spirit thought to influence a man throughout his life   **mortal instruments** human functions (mental and physical; these should obey the genius)   67 **council** intense debate, dispute   **state** condition/commonwealth

    Like to a little kingdom, suffers then
    The nature of an insurrection.

Enter Lucius

70 **LUCIUS** Sir, 'tis your brother Cassius at the door,
    Who doth desire to see you.
BRUTUS Is he alone?
LUCIUS No, sir, there are more with him.
BRUTUS Do you know them?
75 **LUCIUS** No, sir, their hats are plucked about their ears
    And half their faces buried in their cloaks,
    That by no means I may discover them
    By any mark of favour.
BRUTUS Let 'em enter:—   *[Exit Lucius]*
80   They are the faction. O conspiracy,
    Sham'st thou to show thy dang'rous brow by night,
    When evils are most free? O, then, by day
    Where wilt thou find a cavern dark enough
    To mask thy monstrous visage? Seek none,
       conspiracy,
85   Hide it in smiles and affability
    For if thou path thy native semblance on,
    Not Erebus itself were dim enough
    To hide thee from prevention.

Enter the conspirators: Cassius, Casca, Decius, Cinna,
Metellus and Trebonius

CASSIUS I think we are too bold upon your rest:
90   Good morrow, Brutus, do we trouble you?
BRUTUS I have been up this hour, awake all night.
    Know I these men that come along with you?
CASSIUS Yes, every man of them; and no man here
    But honours you, and every one doth wish
95   You had but that opinion of yourself
    Which every noble Roman bears of you.
    This is Trebonius.
BRUTUS He is welcome hither.
CASSIUS This, Decius Brutus.
100 **BRUTUS** He is welcome too.
CASSIUS This, Casca; this, Cinna; and this, Metellus
      Cimber.

---

69 insurrection rebellion **70 brother** brother-in-law; Cassius was married to Brutus' sister **75 plucked about** pulled down over **77 discover** identify **78 mark of favour** facial feature **82 free** unconfined **84 visage** face **86 thou ... on** pursue (i.e. maintain) your natural appearance **87 Erebus** in classical mythology, the dark place through which the dead must pass before they reach the underworld, Hades **88 prevention** being (recognized and) forestalled **89 are too bold** intrude too boldly

BRUTUS They are all welcome.
　　　What watchful cares do interpose themselves
　　　Betwixt your eyes and night?

105　**CASSIUS** Shall I entreat a word?

They whisper

DECIUS Here lies the east: doth not the day break here?

CASCA No.

CINNA O, pardon, sir, it doth; and yon grey lines
　　　That fret the clouds are messengers of day.

110　**CASCA** You shall confess that you are both deceived:
　　　Here, as I point my sword, the sun arises,
　　　Which is a great way growing on the south,
　　　Weighing the youthful season of the year.
　　　Some two months hence, up higher toward the north

115　　He first presents his fire, and the high east
　　　Stands as the Capitol, directly here.

BRUTUS Give me your hands all over, one by one.　　　　*Comes forward*

CASSIUS And let us swear our resolution.　　　　　　*with Cassius*

BRUTUS No, not an oath: if not the face of men,

120　　The sufferance of our souls, the time's abuse;
　　　If these be motives weak, break off betimes,
　　　And every man hence to his idle bed.
　　　So let high-sighted tyranny range on
　　　Till each man drop by lottery. But if these —

125　　As I am sure they do — bear fire enough
　　　To kindle cowards, and to steel with valour
　　　The melting spirits of women, then, countrymen,
　　　What need we any spur but our own cause
　　　To prick us to redress? What other bond

130　　Than secret Romans that have spoke the word
　　　And will not palter? And what other oath
　　　Than honesty to honesty engaged,
　　　That this shall be, or we will fall for it?
　　　Swear priests and cowards, and men cautelous,

135　　Old feeble carrions, and such suffering souls
　　　That welcome wrongs: unto bad causes swear

---

103 watchful cares sleep-preventing anxieties　**104 night** i.e. sleep　**108 yon** yonder, those　**109 fret** adorn, lace　**110 deceived** mistaken　**111 as** i.e. where　**112 growing on** advancing toward　**113 Weighing** considering, taking into account　**117 all over** all of you　**119 face of men** i.e. troubled look of the people　**120 sufferance** suffering　**121 betimes** quickly　**122 idle** unoccupied/lazy　**123 high-sighted** ambitious, with the sight directed upwards/soaring beyond view (image from falconry)　**range** move freely　**124 lottery** chance　**126 steel** make firm　**130 Than** than that of　**secret** trustworthy/concealed　**131 palter** equivocate, use trickery　**132 engaged** pledged, committed　**133 fall** i.e. die　**134 Swear** i.e. those who take oaths are　**cautelous** cautious　**135 carrions** corpses (used here of sick old men)

Such creatures as men doubt. But do not stain
The even virtue of our enterprise,
Nor th'insuppressive mettle of our spirits,
140 To think that or our cause or our performance
Did need an oath, when every drop of blood
That every Roman bears, and nobly bears,
Is guilty of a several bastardy
If he do break the smallest particle
145 Of any promise that hath passed from him.

CASSIUS But what of Cicero? Shall we sound him?
I think he will stand very strong with us.

CASCA Let us not leave him out.

CINNA No, by no means.

150 METELLUS O, let us have him, for his silver hairs
Will purchase us a good opinion,
And buy men's voices to commend our deeds:
It shall be said his judgement ruled our hands.
Our youths and wildness shall no whit appear,
155 But all be buried in his gravity.

BRUTUS O, name him not: let us not break with him,
For he will never follow anything
That other men begin.

CASSIUS Then leave him out.

160 CASCA Indeed, he is not fit.

DECIUS Shall no man else be touched, but only Caesar?

CASSIUS Decius, well urged.— I think it is not meet
Mark Antony, so well beloved of Caesar,
Should outlive Caesar. We shall find of him
165 A shrewd contriver. And you know his means
If he improve them may well stretch so far
As to annoy us all: which to prevent,
Let Antony and Caesar fall together.

BRUTUS Our course will seem too bloody, Caius Cassius,
170 To cut the head off and then hack the limbs —
Like wrath in death and envy afterwards —
For Antony is but a limb of Caesar.
Let's be sacrificers, but not butchers, Caius.

---

137 Such . . . doubt the sort of wretches one can have little faith in   138 even true, steady
139 th'insuppressive the indomitable, not suppressible   140 or either   143 several individual
bastardy i.e. act that shows he is no true, legitimate Roman   146 sound sound out, question   150 silver
hairs i.e. old age/wisdom (silver also suggests money, an image picked up in purchase and buy)
155 gravity sober authority/wisdom   156 break speak, broach the matter   161 touched affected, i.e.
killed   162 meet fitting   165 shrewd contriver cunning schemer/astute strategist   means resources/
power   166 improve exploit, make good use of   167 annoy injure   171 envy malice

We all stand up against the spirit of Caesar,
175   And in the spirit of men there is no blood.
O, that we then could come by Caesar's spirit
And not dismember Caesar! But, alas,
Caesar must bleed for it. And, gentle friends,
Let's kill him boldly, but not wrathfully:
180   Let's carve him as a dish fit for the gods,
Not hew him as a carcass fit for hounds.
And let our hearts, as subtle masters do,
Stir up their servants to an act of rage
And after seem to chide 'em. This shall make
185   Our purpose necessary, and not envious,
Which so appearing to the common eyes,
We shall be called purgers, not murderers.
And for Mark Antony, think not of him,
For he can do no more than Caesar's arm
190   When Caesar's head is off.

CASSIUS   Yet I fear him,
For in the ingrafted love he bears to Caesar —

BRUTUS   Alas, good Cassius, do not think of him:
If he love Caesar, all that he can do
195   Is to himself; take thought and die for Caesar.
And that were much he should, for he is given
To sports, to wildness and much company.

TREBONIUS   There is no fear in him; let him not die,
For he will live and laugh at this hereafter.

Clock strikes

200   BRUTUS   Peace! Count the clock.

CASSIUS   The clock hath stricken three.

TREBONIUS   'Tis time to part.

CASSIUS   But it is doubtful yet
Whether Caesar will come forth today or no,
205   For he is superstitious grown of late,
Quite from the main opinion he held once
Of fantasy, of dreams and ceremonies.
It may be these apparent prodigies,
The unaccustomed terror of this night

---

174 **spirit** influence/essence/disposition   175 **spirit** soul   182 **subtle** cunning   183 **Stir up** provoke
their servants i.e. our hands   184 **chide** rebuke   185 **purpose** purpose seem   187 **purgers** cleansers,
healers (of the state)   192 **ingrafted** firmly implanted (gardening term referring to the practice of grafting a
shoot from one plant onto the stem of another)   195 **take thought** become depressed, sunk in grief
196 **that…should** it would be extreme if he did   198 **no fear** nothing to fear   206 **from the main**
contrary to the solid   207 **ceremonies** ritual divination of omens   208 **apparent** conspicuous, plainly
visible

210 　　　　And the persuasion of his augurers,
　　　　　　May hold him from the Capitol today.
　　　　DECIUS Never fear that. If he be so resolved,
　　　　　　I can o'ersway him, for he loves to hear
　　　　　　That unicorns may be betrayed with trees,
215 　　　　And bears with glasses, elephants with holes,
　　　　　　Lions with toils and men with flatterers.
　　　　　　But when I tell him he hates flatterers,
　　　　　　He says he does, being then most flattered.
　　　　　　Let me work,
220 　　　　For I can give his humour the true bent,
　　　　　　And I will bring him to the Capitol.
　　　　CASSIUS Nay, we will all of us be there to fetch him.
　　　　BRUTUS By the eighth hour. Is that the uttermost?
　　　　CINNA Be that the uttermost, and fail not then.
225 　　　　METELLUS Caius Ligarius doth bear Caesar hard,
　　　　　　Who rated him for speaking well of Pompey.
　　　　　　I wonder none of you have thought of him.
　　　　BRUTUS Now, good Metellus, go along by him:
　　　　　　He loves me well, and I have given him reasons.
230 　　　　Send him but hither and I'll fashion him.
　　　　CASSIUS The morning comes upon's: we'll leave you,
　　　　　　　　Brutus.—
　　　　　　And, friends, disperse yourselves; but all remember
　　　　　　What you have said, and show yourselves true
　　　　　　　　Romans.
　　　　BRUTUS Good gentlemen, look fresh and merrily.
235 　　　　Let not our looks put on our purposes,
　　　　　　But bear it as our Roman actors do,
　　　　　　With untired spirits and formal constancy.
　　　　　　And so good morrow to you every one.—
　　　　　　　　　　　　Exeunt. Brutus remains

　　　　　　Boy! Lucius! Fast asleep? It is no matter.　　　　*Calls*
240 　　　　Enjoy the honey-heavy dew of slumber:
　　　　　　Thou hast no figures, nor no fantasies

210 augurers Roman religious officials who predicted the future by interpreting a variety of signs and portents　**213 o'ersway him** influence him, change his mind　**214 unicorns . . . trees** supposedly the fierce unicorn could be goaded into charging at a tree, where it would become trapped when its horn got embedded in the trunk　**215 glasses** mirrors (into which the bear would gaze, distracted)　**holes** holes in the ground, booby-traps　**216 toils** nets, snares　**220 humour** mood/disposition　**true bent** right inclination, proper direction　**223 uttermost** latest time　**225 bear Caesar hard** bear a grudge towards Caesar, dislike him　**226 rated** reproached, rebuked　**228 by** i.e. to　**229 reasons** i.e. reasons to love me　**230 fashion him** work on him, shape him to our purposes　**231 upon's** upon us　**235 put on** show, reflect　**237 untired** inexhaustible (may play on the sense of 'uncostumed' although this is not historically accurate)　**formal constancy** outward integrity, fidelity to one's role　**241 figures . . . fantasies** imaginings

Which busy care draws in the brains of men;
Therefore thou sleep'st so sound.

Enter Portia

PORTIA Brutus, my lord.

245 **BRUTUS** Portia, what mean you? Wherefore rise you now?
It is not for your health thus to commit
Your weak condition to the raw cold morning.

PORTIA Nor for yours neither. You've ungently, Brutus,
Stole from my bed: and yesternight, at supper,
250 You suddenly arose, and walked about,
Musing, and sighing, with your arms a-cross:
And when I asked you what the matter was,
You stared upon me with ungentle looks.
I urged you further, then you scratched your head,
255 And too impatiently stamped with your foot:
Yet I insisted, yet you answered not,
But with an angry wafture of your hand
Gave sign for me to leave you: so I did,
Fearing to strengthen that impatience
260 Which seemed too much enkindled, and withal
Hoping it was but an effect of humour,
Which sometime hath his hour with every man.
It will not let you eat, nor talk, nor sleep;
And could it work so much upon your shape
265 As it hath much prevailed on your condition,
I should not know you, Brutus. Dear my lord,
Make me acquainted with your cause of grief.

BRUTUS I am not well in health, and that is all.

PORTIA Brutus is wise, and were he not in health,
270 He would embrace the means to come by it.

BRUTUS Why, so I do. Good Portia, go to bed.

PORTIA Is Brutus sick? And is it physical
To walk unbracèd, and suck up the humours
Of the dank morning? What, is Brutus sick?
275 And will he steal out of his wholesome bed
To dare the vile contagion of the night?
And tempt the rheumy and unpurgèd air
To add unto his sickness? No, my Brutus,

---

242 **busy** constantly active/interfering   245 **mean you** are you doing   248 **ungently** unkindly, rudely
251 **arms a-cross** conventional gesture of melancholy or introspection   257 **wafture** (dismissive) wave
260 **withal** in addition   261 **humour** (a bad) mood, (a disordered) temperament   264 **shape** physical
appearance   265 **condition** state of mind   266 **know** recognize   273 **unbracèd** with clothing
unbuttoned   **humours** dampness, noxious vapours   275 **wholesome** healthful   276 **dare** risk/defy
277 **rheumy** moist   **unpurgèd** impure (the sun having yet to purge its moisture)

You have some sick offence within your mind
280   Which by the right and virtue of my place
I ought to know of: and upon my knees   *Kneels*
I charm you, by my once-commended beauty,
By all your vows of love and that great vow
Which did incorporate and make us one,
285   That you unfold to me, your self, your half,
Why you are heavy, and what men tonight
Have had resort to you, for here have been
Some six or seven who did hide their faces
Even from darkness.

290   **BRUTUS** Kneel not, gentle Portia.   *Raises her?*
    PORTIA I should not need, if you were gentle Brutus.   *Rises*
Within the bond of marriage, tell me, Brutus,
Is it excepted I should know no secrets
That appertain to you? Am I your self
295   But as it were in sort or limitation?
To keep with you at meals, comfort your bed
And talk to you sometimes? Dwell I but in the
    suburbs
Of your good pleasure? If it be no more,
Portia is Brutus' harlot, not his wife.
300   **BRUTUS** You are my true and honourable wife,
As dear to me as are the ruddy drops
That visit my sad heart.
    PORTIA If this were true, then should I know this secret.
I grant I am a woman; but withal
305   A woman that Lord Brutus took to wife:
I grant I am a woman; but withal
A woman well-reputed, Cato's daughter.
Think you I am no stronger than my sex
Being so fathered and so husbanded?
310   Tell me your counsels, I will not disclose 'em.
I have made strong proof of my constancy,
Giving myself a voluntary wound
Here in the thigh: can I bear that with patience
And not my husband's secrets?

279 **sick offence** harmful disorder   280 **place** position (as your wife)   282 **charm** conjure, entreat
283 **that great vow** i.e. the marriage vow   285 **unfold** reveal   **half** other half   286 **heavy** sad
287 **resort** access   293 **excepted** made an exception (that)   295 **in … limitation** within certain limits
(legal phrase)   296 **keep** remain   **comfort** make comfortable, bring pleasure to   297 **suburbs** outskirts,
the less tightly regulated parts of a city well-known for prostitution   299 **harlot** prostitute   301 **ruddy**
drops i.e. blood   307 **Cato** Marcus Porcius Cato was known for his rigid moral integrity; as an ally of
Pompey, he committed suicide rather than give in to Caesar   310 **counsels** plans/secrets   311 **constancy**
fortitude

315 **BRUTUS** O ye gods!
  Render me worthy of this noble wife!   *Knock*
  Hark, hark one knocks. Portia, go in awhile,
  And by and by thy bosom shall partake
  The secrets of my heart.
320 All my engagements I will construe to thee,
  All the charactery of my sad brows:
  Leave me with haste.—   *Exit Portia*
  Lucius, who's that knocks?
               Calls
Enter Lucius and Ligarius
         Ligarius wears a kerchief
 LUCIUS Here is a sick man that would speak with you.
325 **BRUTUS** Caius Ligarius, that Metellus spake of.—
  Boy, stand aside.— Caius Ligarius, how?
 LIGARIUS Vouchsafe good morrow from a feeble tongue.
 BRUTUS O, what a time have you chose out, brave Caius,
  To wear a kerchief? Would you were not sick!
330 **LIGARIUS** I am not sick if Brutus have in hand
  Any exploit worthy the name of honour.
 BRUTUS Such an exploit have I in hand, Ligarius,
  Had you a healthful ear to hear of it.
 LIGARIUS By all the gods that Romans bow before,
335 I here discard my sickness. Soul of Rome,   *Takes off the kerchief*
  Brave son, derived from honourable loins,
  Thou like an exorcist hast conjured up
  My mortified spirit. Now bid me run
  And I will strive with things impossible,
340 Yea, get the better of them. What's to do?
 BRUTUS A piece of work that will make sick men whole.
 LIGARIUS But are not some whole that we must make
   sick?
 BRUTUS That must we also. What it is, my Caius,
  I shall unfold to thee as we are going
345 To whom it must be done.
 LIGARIUS Set on your foot,
  And with a heart new-fired I follow you,
  To do I know not what: but it sufficeth
  That Brutus leads me on.   *Thunder*
350 **BRUTUS** Follow me, then.   *Exeunt*

---

318 by and by imminently **bosom** i.e. heart **320 construe** explain **321 charactery** writing, i.e.
meaning **323** *kerchief* scarf generally worn about the head (especially by invalids) **327 Vouchsafe** deign
to accept **337 exorcist** one who calls up spirits by magical rites **338 mortified** deadened (by illness/by
Caesar) **339 strive** contend **341 whole** healthy, well **345 To whom** i.e. to meet the man to whom
346 Set … foot advance, lead on

[Act 2 Scene 2]

Thunder and lightning. Enter Julius Caesar in his nightgown

CAESAR Nor heaven nor earth have been at peace
    tonight:
    Thrice hath Calpurnia in her sleep cried out,
    'Help, ho! They murder Caesar!' Who's within?
Enter a Servant
SERVANT My lord?
5 CAESAR Go bid the priests do present sacrifice
    And bring me their opinions of success.
  SERVANT I will, my lord.   *Exit*
Enter Calpurnia
CALPURNIA What mean you, Caesar? Think you to walk
    forth?
    You shall not stir out of your house today.
10 CAESAR Caesar shall forth. The things that threatened
    me
    Ne'er looked but on my back: when they shall see
    The face of Caesar, they are vanishèd.
  CALPURNIA Caesar, I never stood on ceremonies,
    Yet now they fright me. There is one within,
15 Besides the things that we have heard and seen,
    Recounts most horrid sights seen by the watch.
    A lioness hath whelpèd in the streets,
    And graves have yawned, and yielded up their dead;
    Fierce fiery warriors fight upon the clouds
20 In ranks and squadrons, and right form of war,
    Which drizzled blood upon the Capitol:
    The noise of battle hurtled in the air,
    Horses do neigh, and dying men did groan,
    And ghosts did shriek and squeal about the streets.
25 O Caesar, these things are beyond all use,
    And I do fear them.
  CAESAR What can be avoided
    Whose end is purposed by the mighty gods?
    Yet Caesar shall go forth, for these predictions
30 Are to the world in general as to Caesar.

2.2 *Location: Caesar's house, Rome*   **5 present** immediate   **6 opinions** predictions (based on study of
the entrails of sacrificed animals)   **13 stood on** insisted on, gave weight to   **ceremonies** omens, portents
16 watch night watchmen   **17 whelpèd** given birth   **18 yawned** gaped open   **19 fiery warriors** i.e.
comets, considered to be bad omens   **22 hurtled** clashed noisily   **24 ghosts . . . squeal** ghosts were
traditionally supposed to have thin, high-pitched voices   **25 use** customary experience   **28 end** outcome
purposed determined, intended   **30 to** directed just as much to

CALPURNIA When beggars die there are no comets seen:
    The heavens themselves blaze forth the death of
        princes.
CAESAR Cowards die many times before their deaths,
    The valiant never taste of death but once.
35   Of all the wonders that I yet have heard,
    It seems to me most strange that men should fear,
    Seeing that death, a necessary end,
    Will come when it will come.
Enter a Servant
    What say the augurers?
40 **SERVANT** They would not have you to stir forth today.
    Plucking the entrails of an offering forth,
    They could not find a heart within the beast.
CAESAR The gods do this in shame of cowardice:
    Caesar should be a beast without a heart
45   If he should stay at home today for fear.
    No, Caesar shall not. Danger knows full well
    That Caesar is more dangerous than he.
    We are two lions littered in one day,
    And I the elder and more terrible,
50   And Caesar shall go forth.
CALPURNIA Alas, my lord,
    Your wisdom is consumed in confidence.
    Do not go forth today: call it my fear
    That keeps you in the house, and not your own.
55   We'll send Mark Antony to the senate house,
    And he shall say you are not well today.
    Let me upon my knee prevail in this.   *Kneels*
CAESAR Mark Antony shall say I am not well,
    And for thy humour I will stay at home.   *Raises her?*
Enter Decius
60   Here's Decius Brutus, he shall tell them so.
DECIUS Caesar, all hail. Good morrow, worthy Caesar,
    I come to fetch you to the senate house.
CAESAR And you are come in very happy time
    To bear my greeting to the senators,
65   And tell them that I will not come today:
    Cannot is false, and that I dare not, falser:
    I will not come today. Tell them so, Decius.
CALPURNIA Say he is sick.

---

32 **blaze forth** i.e. proclaim with meteors, fire   **41 of … forth** out of one of the sacrificial animal corpses
43 **in shame of** to shame   **48 littered** born   **52 consumed in** devoured by   **59 humour** whim, fancy
63 **happy** opportune

CAESAR Shall Caesar send a lie?
70   Have I in conquest stretched mine arm so far
        To be afeared to tell greybeards the truth?
        Decius, go tell them Caesar will not come.
    DECIUS Most mighty Caesar, let me know some cause,
        Lest I be laughed at when I tell them so.
75 CAESAR The cause is in my will, I will not come,
        That is enough to satisfy the senate.
        But for your private satisfaction,
        Because I love you, I will let you know.
        Calpurnia here, my wife, stays me at home:
80   She dreamt tonight she saw my statue,
        Which, like a fountain with an hundred spouts,
        Did run pure blood, and many lusty Romans
        Came smiling and did bathe their hands in it.
        And these does she apply for warnings and portents
85   And evils imminent, and on her knee
        Hath begged that I will stay at home today.
    DECIUS This dream is all amiss interpreted.
        It was a vision, fair and fortunate:
        Your statue spouting blood in many pipes
90   In which so many smiling Romans bathed,
        Signifies that from you great Rome shall suck
        Reviving blood, and that great men shall press
        For tinctures, stains, relics and cognizance.
        This by Calpurnia's dream is signified.
95 CAESAR And this way have you well expounded it.
    DECIUS I have, when you have heard what I can say:
        And know it now, the senate have concluded
        To give this day a crown to mighty Caesar.
        If you shall send them word you will not come,
100   Their minds may change. Besides, it were a mock
        Apt to be rendered, for someone to say,
        'Break up the senate till another time
        When Caesar's wife shall meet with better dreams.'
        If Caesar hide himself, shall they not whisper
105   'Lo, Caesar is afraid'?
        Pardon me, Caesar, for my dear, dear love

---

71 greybeards old men (often derogatory)   79 stays detains   82 lusty vigorous, lively, eager   84 apply for interpret as   87 amiss wrongly   92 press appeal/crowd forward   93 tinctures, stains, relics i.e. tokens marked with a martyr's blood (tinctures also includes the sense 'colours on a coat of arms') cognizance tokens/heraldic badge worn by a nobleman's servant   100 were … rendered would be a likely joke

    To our proceeding bids me tell you this,
    And reason to my love is liable.
CAESAR How foolish do your fears seem now,
      Calpurnia?
110   I am ashamèd I did yield to them.
    Give me my robe, for I will go.
Enter Brutus, Ligarius, Metellus, Casca, Trebonius, Cinna
and Publius
    And look where Publius is come to fetch me.
PUBLIUS Good morrow, Caesar.
CAESAR Welcome, Publius.—
115   What, Brutus, are you stirred so early too?—
    Good morrow, Casca.— Caius Ligarius,
    Caesar was ne'er so much your enemy
    As that same ague which hath made you lean.—
    What is't o'clock?
120 **BRUTUS** Caesar, 'tis strucken eight.
CAESAR I thank you for your pains and courtesy.
Enter Antony
    See, Antony, that revels long o'nights,
Is notwithstanding up.— Good morrow, Antony.
ANTONY So to most noble Caesar.
125 **CAESAR** Bid them prepare within: *To Calpurnia or to a Servant*
    I am to blame to be thus waited for.—
                [Exit Calpurnia or a Servant]
    Now, Cinna, now, Metellus, what, Trebonius,
    I have an hour's talk in store for you.
    Remember that you call on me today:
130   Be near me, that I may remember you.
TREBONIUS Caesar, I will:— and so near will I be   *Aside*
    That your best friends shall wish I had been
      further.
CAESAR Good friends, go in, and taste some wine with
      me,
    And we, like friends, will straightway go together.
135 **BRUTUS** That every like is not the same, O Caesar,   *Aside*
    The heart of Brutus earns to think upon.   *Exeunt*

---

108 reason … liable decorum is overruled by my love **118 ague** fever, sickness **123 notwithstanding up** nevertheless out of bed **130 remember** acknowledge, reward **135 That … same** i.e. the fact that those who behave **like friends** may not actually be so **136 earns** grieves

[Act 2 Scene 3]   *running scene 4*

Enter Artemidorus   *Reading a paper*

ARTEMIDORUS 'Caesar, beware of Brutus, take heed of
          Cassius, come not near Casca, have an eye to Cinna,
          trust not Trebonius, mark well Metellus Cimber,
          Decius Brutus loves thee not, thou hast wronged
5   Caius Ligarius. There is but one mind in all these
          men, and it is bent against Caesar. If thou be'st not
          immortal, look about you: security gives way to
          conspiracy. The mighty gods defend thee. Thy lover,
          Artemidorus.'
10   Here will I stand till Caesar pass along,
          And as a suitor will I give him this.
          My heart laments that virtue cannot live
          Out of the teeth of emulation.
          If thou read this, O Caesar, thou mayst live;
15   If not, the Fates with traitors do contrive.   *Exit*

[Act 2 Scene 4]   *running scene 5*

Enter Portia and Lucius

PORTIA I prithee, boy, run to the senate house.
          Stay not to answer me, but get thee gone.
          Why dost thou stay?
LUCIUS To know my errand, madam.
5   PORTIA I would have had thee there and here again
          Ere I can tell thee what thou shouldst do there.—
          O constancy, be strong upon my side,   *Aside*
          Set a huge mountain 'tween my heart and tongue:
          I have a man's mind, but a woman's might.
10   How hard it is for women to keep counsel.—
          Art thou here yet?
LUCIUS Madam, what should I do?
          Run to the Capitol, and nothing else?
          And so return to you, and nothing else?
15   PORTIA Yes, bring me word, boy, if thy lord look well,
          For he went sickly forth: and take good note

2.3 *Location: a street near the Capitol, Rome*   **6 bent** resolved/directed   **7 security** over-confidence,
complacency   **way** opportunity/access   **8 lover** dear and loyal friend   **11 suitor** petitioner   **13 Out of**
free from   **teeth** i.e. bite   **emulation** ambitious rivalry   **15 contrive** plot, conspire   2.4 *Location:*
outside Brutus' house, Rome   **7 constancy** resolution, fortitude   **9 man's** i.e. strong, virtuous
10 counsel secrets   **16 take good note** observe closely

What Caesar doth, what suitors press to him.
Hark, boy, what noise is that?
LUCIUS I hear none, madam.

20   PORTIA Prithee listen well:
I heard a bustling rumour like a fray,
And the wind brings it from the Capitol.
LUCIUS Sooth, madam, I hear nothing.

Enter the Soothsayer

PORTIA Come hither, fellow. Which way hast thou
been?

25   SOOTHSAYER At mine own house, good lady.
PORTIA What is't o'clock?
SOOTHSAYER About the ninth hour, lady.
PORTIA Is Caesar yet gone to the Capitol?
SOOTHSAYER Madam, not yet. I go to take my stand

30   To see him pass on to the Capitol.
PORTIA Thou hast some suit to Caesar, hast thou not?
SOOTHSAYER That I have, lady, if it will please Caesar
To be so good to Caesar as to hear me:
I shall beseech him to befriend himself.

35   PORTIA Why, know'st thou any harm's intended
towards him?
SOOTHSAYER None that I know will be
Much that I fear may chance.
Good morrow to you. Here the street is narrow:
The throng that follows Caesar at the heels,

40   Of senators, of praetors, common suitors,
Will crowd a feeble man almost to death:
I'll get me to a place more void, and there
Speak to great Caesar as he comes along.   *Exit*
PORTIA I must go in. Ay me! How weak a thing

45   The heart of woman is.— O Brutus,
The heavens speed thee in thine enterprise.—
Sure, the boy heard me. Brutus hath a suit
That Caesar will not grant. O, I grow faint.—
Run, Lucius, and commend me to my lord,

50   Say I am merry. Come to me again,
And bring me word what he doth say to thee.
Exeunt [separately]

---

21 **bustling rumour** agitated commotion   **fray** fight, noisy brawl/din, stir   23 **Sooth** in truth   31 **suit**
petition, formal request   34 **befriend** i.e. help, protect   40 **praetors** magistrates (of whom Brutus is
one)   42 **void** empty   46 **speed** prosper   49 **commend me** convey my greetings

Act 3 [Scene 1]

running scene 6

Flourish. Enter Caesar, Brutus, Cassius, Casca, Decius,
Metellus, Trebonius, Cinna, Antony, Lepidus, Artemidorus,
Publius [Popilius Lena] and the Soothsayer

CAESAR The Ides of March are come. *To the Soothsayer*
SOOTHSAYER Ay, Caesar, but not gone.
ARTEMIDORUS Hail, Caesar. Read this schedule.
DECIUS Trebonius doth desire you to o'erread —
5   At your best leisure — this his humble suit.
ARTEMIDORUS O Caesar, read mine first, for mine's a suit
    That touches Caesar nearer. Read it, great Caesar.
CAESAR What touches us ourself shall be last served.
ARTEMIDORUS Delay not, Caesar, read it instantly.
10 CAESAR What, is the fellow mad?
PUBLIUS Sirrah, give place. *To Artemidorus*
CASSIUS What, urge you your petitions in the street?
    Come to the Capitol. *Caesar and his train move on*
POPILIUS I wish your enterprise today may thrive. *To Cassius*
15 CASSIUS What enterprise, Popilius?
POPILIUS Fare you well. *Moves toward Caesar*
BRUTUS What said Popilius Lena?
CASSIUS He wished today our enterprise might thrive:
    I fear our purpose is discoverèd.
20 BRUTUS Look how he makes to Caesar: mark him.
CASSIUS Casca, be sudden, for we fear prevention.
    Brutus, what shall be done? If this be known,
    Cassius or Caesar never shall turn back,
    For I will slay myself.
25 BRUTUS Cassius, be constant:
    Popilius Lena speaks not of our purposes,
    For look, he smiles, and Caesar doth not change.
CASSIUS Trebonius knows his time: for look you, Brutus.
    He draws Mark Antony out of the way.
              [Exeunt Antony and Trebonius]
30 DECIUS Where is Metellus Cimber? Let him go *Caesar sits?*
    And presently prefer his suit to Caesar.
BRUTUS He is addressed: press near and second him.

3.1 *Location: on the way to and then within the Capitol, Rome*   **3 schedule** document   **4 o'erread**
read over   **7 touches Caesar nearer** affects Caesar more directly   **8 served** seen to, addressed/formally
delivered (legal term)   **11 Sirrah** sir (term of address used to a social inferior)   **place** way   **20 makes to**
approaches   **21 sudden** swift   **prevention** interruption, intervention   **23 turn back** return (alive)
25 constant steady, controlled   **27 Caesar** i.e. Caesar's expression   **31 prefer** advance, promote
32 addressed prepared   **second** support

CINNA Casca, you are the first that rears your hand.
CAESAR Are we all ready? What is now amiss
35   That Caesar and his senate must redress?
METELLUS Most high, most mighty and most puissant
        Caesar,   *Comes forward*
        Metellus Cimber throws before thy seat   *Kneels*
        An humble heart—
CAESAR I must prevent thee, Cimber.
40   These couchings and these lowly courtesies
        Might fire the blood of ordinary men,
        And turn pre-ordinance and first decree
        Into the lane of children. Be not fond
        To think that Caesar bears such rebel blood
45   That will be thawed from the true quality
        With that which melteth fools — I mean sweet
            words,
        Low-crookèd curtsies and base spaniel-fawning.
        Thy brother by decree is banishèd:
        If thou dost bend and pray and fawn for him,
50   I spurn thee like a cur out of my way.
        Know, Caesar doth not wrong, nor without cause
        Will he be satisfied.
METELLUS Is there no voice more worthy than my own
        To sound more sweetly in great Caesar's ear
55   For the repealing of my banished brother?
BRUTUS I kiss thy hand, but not in flattery, Caesar,   *Kneels*
        Desiring thee that Publius Cimber may
        Have an immediate freedom of repeal.
CAESAR What, Brutus?
60 CASSIUS Pardon, Caesar: Caesar, pardon.
        As low as to thy foot doth Cassius fall,   *Kneels*
        To beg enfranchisement for Publius Cimber.
CAESAR I could be well moved if I were as you:
        If I could pray to move, prayers would move me.

---

33 rears raises up   36 puissant powerful   37 seat chair of state/high status   40 These couchings this
bowing, stooping   lowly courtesies humble (or 'low') bows   41 fire excite/incite to action
42 turn...lane cast...into the path/return (or transform)...to the narrow understanding: lane may be a
variant of 'line' (i.e. 'rule') though many editors emend to 'law'   pre-ordinance...decree previously
established and fundamental laws   43 fond (so) foolish   44 rebel blood i.e. blood that will revolt against
reason   45 quality nature, property/excellence   46 sweet flattering, sugary   47 Low-crooked with body
and knee bent low (both 'low' and 'crooked' have connotations of dishonesty)   spaniel-fawning dog-like
fawning (spaniels were proverbially submissive)   49 pray beg   50 spurn kick   cur dog   51 cause good
reason   52 satisfied convinced (to grant a pardon)   55 repealing recalling (from exile)   58 freedom of
repeal permission to be recalled/freedom resulting from being recalled   62 enfranchisement liberation
64 pray to move plead with others to act

65 But I am constant as the northern star,
Of whose true-fixed and resting quality
There is no fellow in the firmament.
The skies are painted with unnumbered sparks,
They are all fire and every one doth shine:
70 But there's but one in all doth hold his place.
So in the world: 'tis furnished well with men,
And men are flesh and blood, and apprehensive;
Yet in the number I do know but one
That unassailable holds on his rank,
75 Unshaked of motion. And that I am he,
Let me a little show it, even in this:
That I was constant Cimber should be banished,
And constant do remain to keep him so.
CINNA O Caesar—   *Kneels*
80 CAESAR Hence. Wilt thou lift up Olympus?
DECIUS Great Caesar—   *About to kneel*
CAESAR Doth not Brutus bootless kneel?
CASCA Speak hands for me!
They stab Caesar   *Casca first, Brutus last*
CAESAR *Et tu, Bruté?*— Then fall, Caesar.   *Dies*
85 CINNA Liberty! Freedom! Tyranny is dead!
Run hence, proclaim, cry it about the streets.
CASSIUS Some to the common pulpits and cry out   *In the ensuing tumult,*
'Liberty, freedom and enfranchisement!'   *exeunt all but the*
BRUTUS People and senators, be not affrighted.   *conspirators and Publius*
90 Fly not, stand still: ambition's debt is paid.
CASCA Go to the pulpit, Brutus.
DECIUS And Cassius too.
BRUTUS Where's Publius?
CINNA Here, quite confounded with this mutiny.
95 METELLUS Stand fast together, lest some friend of
Caesar's
Should chance—

---

65 **northern star** the only star in the sky which does not appear to move when viewed from earth
66 **resting** unchanging, stable   67 **fellow** counterpart, equal   **firmament** sky   68 **sparks** i.e. stars
72 **apprehensive** capable of perception and understanding   74 **holds . . . rank** maintains his position
75 **of motion** by movement of his own/by the persuasions of others   80 **Hence** be gone   **Olympus** in
Greek mythology, the mountain home of the gods   82 **bootless** pointlessly, uselessly   83 **hands** i.e. his
own hands; perhaps also those of the other conspirators   84 *Et tu, Bruté?* 'And you (too), Brutus?'
(Latin)   87 **common pulpits** public speaking platforms   89 **affrighted** frightened   90 **ambition's . . .**
paid i.e. the price for Caesar's ambition has been paid with his death (and no one else will be harmed)
94 **confounded with** dumbfounded, confused by   **mutiny** chaos/revolt   95 **fast** firm

BRUTUS Talk not of standing. Publius, good cheer:
       There is no harm intended to your person,
       Nor to no Roman else: so tell them, Publius.
100   **CASSIUS** And leave us, Publius, lest that the people,
       Rushing on us, should do your age some mischief.
       BRUTUS Do so, and let no man abide this deed
       But we the doers.   [*Exit Publius*]
       Enter Trebonius
       CASSIUS Where is Antony?
105   **TREBONIUS** Fled to his house amazed.
       Men, wives and children stare, cry out and run
       As it were doomsday.
       BRUTUS Fates, we will know your pleasures.
       That we shall die we know: 'tis but the time
110   And drawing days out that men stand upon.
       CASCA Why, he that cuts off twenty years of life
       Cuts off so many years of fearing death.
       BRUTUS Grant that, and then is death a benefit:
       So are we Caesar's friends that have abridged
115   His time of fearing death. Stoop, Romans, stoop,
       And let us bathe our hands in Caesar's blood
       Up to the elbows and besmear our swords:
       Then walk we forth, even to the market-place,   *They smear their*
       And waving our red weapons o'er our heads,   *hands and weapons*
120   Let's all cry 'Peace, freedom and liberty!'   *with Caesar's blood*
       CASSIUS Stoop, then, and wash. How many ages
             hence
       Shall this our lofty scene be acted over,
       In states unborn and accents yet unknown?
       BRUTUS How many times shall Caesar bleed in sport
125   That now on Pompey's basis lies along
       No worthier than the dust?
       CASSIUS So oft as that shall be,
       So often shall the knot of us be called
       The men that gave their country liberty.
130   **DECIUS** What, shall we forth?

97 standing making a stand   good cheer cheer up, be heartened   101 age elderly personage   mischief
injury, harm   102 abide pay the penalty for/remain with   105 amazed stunned/dismayed/alarmed
107 As as if   108 pleasures wills   109 time i.e. time of death   110 drawing days out prolonging of
life   stand upon are uncertain about/attach importance to/demand to know   118 market-place i.e. the
Forum, centre of public life   122 acted over acted out/acted over again   123 accents languages
125 Pompey's basis the pedestal of Pompey's statue   along stretched out   128 knot group

CASSIUS Ay, every man away.
　　Brutus shall lead, and we will grace his heels
　　With the most boldest and best hearts of Rome.
Enter a Servant
BRUTUS Soft, who comes here? A friend of Antony's.
135　SERVANT Thus, Brutus, did my master bid me kneel,　　　　　*Kneels*
　　Thus did Mark Antony bid me fall down,
　　And being prostrate thus he bade me say:
　　Brutus is noble, wise, valiant and honest;
　　Caesar was mighty, bold, royal and loving.
140　Say I love Brutus and I honour him,
　　Say I feared Caesar, honoured him and loved him.
　　If Brutus will vouchsafe that Antony
　　May safely come to him and be resolved
　　How Caesar hath deserved to lie in death,
145　Mark Antony shall not love Caesar dead
　　So well as Brutus living, but will follow
　　The fortunes and affairs of noble Brutus
　　Thorough the hazards of this untrod state
　　With all true faith. So says my master Antony.
150　BRUTUS Thy master is a wise and valiant Roman:
　　I never thought him worse.
　　Tell him, so please him come unto this place,
　　He shall be satisfied, and by my honour
　　Depart untouched.
155　SERVANT I'll fetch him presently.　　　　*Exit Servant*
　　BRUTUS I know that we shall have him well to friend.
　　CASSIUS I wish we may: but yet have I a mind
　　　　That fears him much, and my misgiving still
　　　　Falls shrewdly to the purpose.
Enter Antony
160　BRUTUS But here comes Antony.— Welcome, Mark
　　　　Antony.
　　ANTONY O mighty Caesar! Dost thou lie so low?　　　*To the body*
　　Are all thy conquests, glories, triumphs, spoils,
　　Shrunk to this little measure? Fare thee well.—
　　I know not, gentlemen, what you intend,

---

132 grace honour (by following)   134 Soft wait a moment   138 honest honourable   141 feared felt
reverence and awe for   142 vouchsafe permit, grant   143 be resolved learn   148 Thorough
through   untrod state unprecedented state of affairs   149 faith loyalty, constancy   153 satisfied
informed, reassured, convinced   154 untouched unharmed   155 presently immediately   156 well to as
a good   157 wish hope   mind feeling, presentiment   158 fears doubts, mistrusts   still...purpose
always proves horribly accurate   shrewdly astutely/seriously/dangerously   162 spoils plunder of war
163 measure extent, quantity

165   Who else must be let blood, who else is rank:
     If I myself, there is no hour so fit
     As Caesar's death's hour, nor no instrument
     Of half that worth as those your swords, made rich
     With the most noble blood of all this world.
170   I do beseech ye, if you bear me hard,
     Now, whilst your purpled hands do reek and smoke,
     Fulfil your pleasure. Live a thousand years,
     I shall not find myself so apt to die.
     No place will please me so, no mean of death,
175   As here by Caesar, and by you cut off,
     The choice and master spirits of this age.
  BRUTUS O Antony! Beg not your death of us:
     Though now we must appear bloody and cruel,
     As by our hands and this our present act
180   You see we do, yet see you but our hands
     And this the bleeding business they have done:
     Our hearts you see not: they are pitiful,
     And pity to the general wrong of Rome —
     As fire drives out fire, so pity pity —
185   Hath done this deed on Caesar. For your part,
     To you our swords have leaden points, Mark Antony:
     Our arms in strength of malice, and our hearts
     Of brothers' temper, do receive you in
     With all kind love, good thoughts and reverence.
190   CASSIUS Your voice shall be as strong as any man's
     In the disposing of new dignities.
  BRUTUS Only be patient till we have appeased
     The multitude, beside themselves with fear,
     And then we will deliver you the cause
195   Why I, that did love Caesar when I struck him,
     Have thus proceeded.
  ANTONY I doubt not of your wisdom.
     Let each man render me his bloody hand.—   *Shakes hands with each*
     First, Marcus Brutus, will I shake with you;—   *of them in turn*

---

165 be let blood i.e. killed (literally, 'bled' as a doctor's patient was)   **rank** diseased/swollen   **171 purpled** blood-red   **reek** steam (with hot blood)   **172 Live** were I to live   **173 apt** ready, prepared   **174 mean** manner   **175 cut off** killed   **176 choice** best, most worthy   **master** leading   **180 see you but** you only see   **182 pitiful** full of pity, merciful   **184 pity pity** i.e. our pity for Rome drove out pity for Caesar   **186 leaden** dull, blunt, i.e. benign   **187 in . . . malice** though strongly hostile to Caesar/though strong with the power to harm   **188 Of brothers' temper** with brotherly temperament   **receive** admit, embrace   **189 kind** gentle, well-meaning/brotherly, natural   **190 voice** vote   **191 disposing** distribution **dignities** offices of state, formal roles   **193 multitude** common people   **194 deliver you** inform you of **cause** reason (plays on the sense of 'grounds for legal action')   **196 proceeded** taken action (plays on the sense of 'taken legal action')   **198 render** give

200 Next, Caius Cassius, do I take your hand;—
     Now, Decius Brutus, yours;— now yours, Metellus;—
     Yours, Cinna;— and my valiant Casca, yours;—
     Though last, not least in love, yours, good
        Trebonius.—
     Gentlemen all: alas, what shall I say?
205 My credit now stands on such slipp'ry ground
     That one of two bad ways you must conceit me,
     Either a coward or a flatterer.—
     That I did love thee, Caesar, O, 'tis true:
     If then thy spirit look upon us now,
210 Shall it not grieve thee dearer than thy death
     To see thy Antony making his peace,
     Shaking the bloody fingers of thy foes?
     Most noble in the presence of thy corpse,
     Had I as many eyes as thou hast wounds,
215 Weeping as fast as they stream forth thy blood,
     It would become me better than to close
     In terms of friendship with thine enemies.
     Pardon me, Julius! Here wast thou bayed, brave hart,
     Here didst thou fall, and here thy hunters stand
220 Signed in thy spoil and crimsoned in thy Lethe.—
     O world, thou wast the forest to this hart,
     And this indeed, O world, the heart of thee.—
     How like a deer, strucken by many princes,
     Dost thou here lie?
225 **CASSIUS** Mark Antony—
     ANTONY Pardon me, Caius Cassius.
        The enemies of Caesar shall say this:
        Then, in a friend, it is cold modesty.
     CASSIUS I blame you not for praising Caesar so,
230 But what compact mean you to have with us?
        Will you be pricked in number of our friends,
        Or shall we on, and not depend on you?
     ANTONY Therefore I took your hands, but was indeed
        Swayed from the point by looking down on Caesar.
235 Friends am I with you all, and love you all,

---

205 credit credibility/reputation   **slipp'ry** perhaps also literally, due to Caesar's blood   **206 conceit** think
of   **210 dearer** more acutely   **213 Most noble** addressed to Caesar's spirit   **216 become** befit, suit
close come to an agreement, unite   **218 bayed** hunted by dogs until cornered   **hart** male deer; puns on
'heart'   **220 Signed in** marked with   **spoil** slaughter, (blood of your) mangled body   **Lethe** the river of
Hades, the classical underworld, which induced forgetfulness; here refers to Caesar's death/oblivion
222 this i.e. this hart, Caesar   **227 The enemies** even the enemies   **228 cold modesty** sober
moderation   **230 compact** agreement   **231 pricked** marked down   **232 on** proceed   **233 Therefore** for
that reason (i.e. to be counted as a friend)

Upon this hope, that you shall give me reasons
Why and wherein Caesar was dangerous.

BRUTUS Or else were this a savage spectacle:
Our reasons are so full of good regard
240   That were you, Antony, the son of Caesar,
You should be satisfied.

ANTONY That's all I seek,
And am moreover suitor, that I may
Produce his body to the market-place,
245   And in the pulpit, as becomes a friend,
Speak in the order of his funeral.

BRUTUS You shall, Mark Antony.

CASSIUS Brutus, a word with you.
You know not what you do. Do not consent   *Aside to Brutus*
250   That Antony speak in his funeral:
Know you how much the people may be moved
By that which he will utter.

BRUTUS By your pardon: *Aside to Cassius*
I will myself into the pulpit first,
255   And show the reason of our Caesar's death.
What Antony shall speak, I will protest
He speaks by leave and by permission,
And that we are contented Caesar shall
Have all true rites and lawful ceremonies.
260   It shall advantage more than do us wrong.

CASSIUS I know not what may fall. I like it not.   *Aside to Brutus*

BRUTUS Mark Antony, here take you Caesar's body.
You shall not in your funeral speech blame us,
But speak all good you can devise of Caesar,
265   And say you do't by our permission:
Else shall you not have any hand at all
About his funeral. And you shall speak
In the same pulpit whereto I am going,
After my speech is ended.

270   **ANTONY** Be it so:
I do desire no more.

BRUTUS Prepare the body then, and follow us.
                              Exeunt. Antony remains

ANTONY O, pardon me, thou bleeding piece of earth,   *To Caesar's body*
That I am meek and gentle with these butchers.
275   Thou art the ruins of the noblest man

---

238 Or else otherwise   239 good regard just consideration   244 Produce bring forth   246 order
ceremony   256 protest declare   257 leave permission, consent   259 true rites proper funeral rites
261 fall befall, happen   267 About i.e. in

That ever livèd in the tide of times.
Woe to the hand that shed this costly blood.
Over thy wounds now do I prophesy —
Which like dumb mouths do ope their ruby lips
280 To beg the voice and utterance of my tongue —
A curse shall light upon the limbs of men:
Domestic fury and fierce civil strife
Shall cumber all the parts of Italy:
Blood and destruction shall be so in use,
285 And dreadful objects so familiar,
That mothers shall but smile when they behold
Their infants quartered with the hands of war:
All pity choked with custom of fell deeds,
And Caesar's spirit ranging for revenge,
290 With Ate by his side, come hot from hell,
Shall in these confines, with a monarch's voice
Cry havoc and let slip the dogs of war,
That this foul deed shall smell above the earth
With carrion men, groaning for burial.—

Enter Octavius' Servant

295   You serve Octavius Caesar, do you not?
SERVANT I do, Mark Antony.
ANTONY Caesar did write for him to come to Rome.
SERVANT He did receive his letters and is coming,
And bid me say to you by word of mouth—
300   O Caesar!   *Sees the body*
ANTONY Thy heart is big: get thee apart and weep.
Passion, I see, is catching, for mine eyes,
Seeing those beads of sorrow stand in thine,
Began to water. Is thy master coming?
305 **SERVANT** He lies tonight within seven leagues of Rome.
ANTONY Post back with speed and tell him what hath
         chanced:
Here is a mourning Rome, a dangerous Rome,
No Rome of safety for Octavius yet.
Hie hence, and tell him so. Yet stay awhile.
310   Thou shalt not back till I have borne this corpse

---

276 **tide of times** course of history   277 **costly** dear, precious   283 **cumber** overwhelm, destroy/trouble, burden   284 **in use** commonplace, customary   285 **objects** sights   287 **quartered with** cut to pieces by   288 **custom of** constant exposure to   **fell** cruel, fierce   289 **ranging** roving, roaming   290 **Ate** Greek goddess of discord and vengeance   291 **confines** regions   292 **havoc** war cry signalling merciless slaughter   **let slip** unleash   293 **That** so that   **foul** wicked/stinking   294 **With** i.e. along with   **carrion men** rotting carcasses/corrupt men   **groaning** crying out   301 **big** swollen (with grief)   302 **Passion** grief, strong emotion   305 **seven leagues** twenty-one miles   306 **Post** ride quickly   309 **Hie hence** hurry away

Into the market-place: there shall I try
In my oration how the people take
The cruel issue of these bloody men,
According to the which thou shalt discourse
315   To young Octavius of the state of things.
Lend me your hand.   *Exeunt*   **With the body**

[Act 3 Scene 2]

running scene 7

*Enter Brutus and goes into the pulpit, and Cassius with the
Plebeians*

PLEBEIANS We will be satisfied: let us be satisfied.
BRUTUS Then follow me, and give me audience, friends.
      Cassius, go you into the other street
      And part the numbers:
5   Those that will hear me speak, let 'em stay here;
      Those that will follow Cassius, go with him
      And public reasons shall be renderèd
      Of Caesar's death.
FIRST PLEBEIAN I will hear Brutus speak.
10   SECOND PLEBEIAN I will hear Cassius, and compare their
            reasons
      When severally we hear them renderèd.
                      [*Exit Cassius, with some of the Plebeians*]
THIRD PLEBEIAN The noble Brutus is ascended: silence!
BRUTUS Be patient till the last.
      Romans, countrymen, and lovers, hear me for my
15   cause and be silent, that you may hear. Believe me
      for mine honour and have respect to mine honour,
      that you may believe. Censure me in your wisdom
      and awake your senses, that you may the better
      judge. If there be any in this assembly, any dear
20   friend of Caesar's, to him I say that Brutus' love to
      Caesar was no less than his. If then that friend
      demand why Brutus rose against Caesar, this is my
      answer: not that I loved Caesar less, but that I loved
      Rome more. Had you rather Caesar were living, and
25   die all slaves, than that Caesar were dead, to live all
      free men? As Caesar loved me, I weep for him; as he

---

311 **try** test   313 **issue** outcome (of the deed)   314 **which** results of which   **discourse** relate
3.2 *Location: the Roman Forum*   2 **give me audience** listen to me   4 **part the numbers** divide the
crowd   7 **public** given in public/concerning the public   **renderèd** given   11 **severally** separately
13 **last** end (of my speech)   14 **lovers** friends   15 **cause** grounds for action/explanation/subject of concern
16 **for** because of   17 **Censure** judge   18 **senses** minds, wits

was fortunate, I rejoice at it; as he was valiant, I
honour him: but as he was ambitious, I slew him.
There is tears, for his love: joy, for his fortune:
30 honour, for his valour: and death, for his ambition.
Who is here so base, that would be a bondman? If
any, speak, for him have I offended. Who is here so
rude, that would not be a Roman? If any, speak, for
him have I offended. Who is here so vile, that will not
35 love his country? If any, speak, for him have I
offended. I pause for a reply.

ALL None, Brutus, none.

BRUTUS Then none have I offended. I have done no
more to Caesar, than you shall do to Brutus. The
40 question of his death is enrolled in the Capitol: his
glory not extenuated, wherein he was worthy, nor
his offences enforced, for which he suffered death.

Enter Mark Antony with Caesar's body

Here comes his body, mourned by Mark Antony,
who, though he had no hand in his death, shall
45 receive the benefit of his dying, a place in the
commonwealth, as which of you shall not? With this
I depart, that as I slew my best lover for the good of
Rome, I have the same dagger for myself, when it
shall please my country to need my death.   *Comes down from*
the pulpit

50 ALL Live Brutus, live, live!

FIRST PLEBEIAN Bring him with triumph home unto his
house.

SECOND PLEBEIAN Give him a statue with his ancestors.

THIRD PLEBEIAN Let him be Caesar.

55 FOURTH PLEBEIAN Caesar's better parts
Shall be crowned in Brutus.

FIRST PLEBEIAN We'll bring him to his house with shouts
and clamours.

BRUTUS My countrymen—

60 SECOND PLEBEIAN Peace, silence, Brutus speaks.

FIRST PLEBEIAN Peace, ho.

BRUTUS Good countrymen, let me depart alone,
And, for my sake, stay here with Antony:

---

33 **rude** uncivilized   34 **vile** lowly, contemptible   40 **question of** considerations behind   **enrolled**
officially recorded   41 **extenuated** lessened, minimized   42 **enforced** exaggerated, emphasized
45 **place . . . commonwealth** i.e. his rights as a free man in the Roman republic   51 **triumph** pomp,
ceremony   53 **SECOND PLEBEIAN** not the same man who left earlier to hear Cassius   55 **parts**
qualities   56 **crowned** literally crowned/rewarded/surpassed

                Do grace to Caesar's corpse and grace his speech
65   Tending to Caesar's glories, which Mark Antony —
            By our permission — is allowed to make.
            I do entreat you, not a man depart
            Save I alone, till Antony have spoke.   *Exit*
        FIRST PLEBEIAN Stay, ho, and let us hear Mark Antony.
70   **THIRD PLEBEIAN** Let him go up into the public chair.
            We'll hear him.— Noble Antony, go up.
        ANTONY For Brutus' sake I am beholding to you.   *Goes into the pulpit*
        FOURTH PLEBEIAN What does he say of Brutus?
        THIRD PLEBEIAN He says, for Brutus' sake
75   He finds himself beholding to us all.
        FOURTH PLEBEIAN 'Twere best he speak no harm of
                Brutus here.
        FIRST PLEBEIAN This Caesar was a tyrant.
        THIRD PLEBEIAN Nay, that's certain:
            We are blest that Rome is rid of him.
80   **SECOND PLEBEIAN** Peace, let us hear what Antony can
                say.
        ANTONY You gentle Romans.
        ALL Peace, ho, let us hear him.
        ANTONY Friends, Romans, countrymen, lend me your
                ears:
            I come to bury Caesar, not to praise him.
85   The evil that men do lives after them:
            The good is oft interrèd with their bones.
            So let it be with Caesar. The noble Brutus
            Hath told you Caesar was ambitious:
            If it were so, it was a grievous fault,
90   And grievously hath Caesar answered it.
            Here, under leave of Brutus and the rest —
            For Brutus is an honourable man:
            So are they all, all honourable men —
            Come I to speak in Caesar's funeral.
95   He was my friend, faithful and just to me;
            But Brutus says, he was ambitious,
            And Brutus is an honourable man.
            He hath brought many captives home to Rome,
            Whose ransoms did the general coffers fill:
100   Did this in Caesar seem ambitious?
            When that the poor have cried, Caesar hath wept:

---

64 Do grace to honour, respect   **grace** listen courteously to   **65 Tending** relating   **70 public chair**
pulpit, platform for public orations   **72 beholding** obliged, indebted   **86 interrèd** buried   **90 answered**
paid for   **91 leave** permission   **99 general coffers** public treasury

Ambition should be made of sterner stuff.
Yet Brutus says, he was ambitious,
And Brutus is an honourable man.

105 You all did see, that on the Lupercal,
I thrice presented him a kingly crown,
Which he did thrice refuse. Was this ambition?
Yet Brutus says, he was ambitious,
And sure he is an honourable man.

110 I speak not to disprove what Brutus spoke,
But here I am, to speak what I do know.
You all did love him once, not without cause:
What cause withholds you then, to mourn for
    him?—
O judgement! Thou art fled to brutish beasts

115 And men have lost their reason.— Bear with me:
My heart is in the coffin there with Caesar,
And I must pause till it come back to me.

FIRST PLEBEIAN Methinks there is much reason in his
    sayings.

SECOND PLEBEIAN If thou consider rightly of the matter,
120   Caesar has had great wrong.

THIRD PLEBEIAN Has he, masters?
    I fear there will a worse come in his place.

FOURTH PLEBEIAN Marked ye his words? He would not
    take the crown:
    Therefore 'tis certain he was not ambitious.

125 **FIRST PLEBEIAN** If it be found so, some will dear abide it.

SECOND PLEBEIAN Poor soul, his eyes are red as fire with
    weeping.

THIRD PLEBEIAN There's not a nobler man in Rome than
    Antony.

FOURTH PLEBEIAN Now mark him, he begins again to
    speak.

ANTONY But yesterday the word of Caesar might
130 Have stood against the world: now lies he there,
    And none so poor to do him reverence.
    O masters! If I were disposed to stir
    Your hearts and minds to mutiny and rage,
    I should do Brutus wrong, and Cassius wrong,
135 Who — you all know — are honourable men.
    I will not do them wrong: I rather choose

121 masters sirs   **122 worse** i.e. worse tyrant   **125 dear abide it** suffer grievously for it   **129 But** only   **130 stood against** resisted, fought against   **131 poor** humble

To wrong the dead, to wrong myself and you,
Than I will wrong such honourable men.
But here's a parchment, with the seal of Caesar.   *Shows the will*
140   I found it in his closet: 'tis his will.
Let but the commons hear this testament —
Which, pardon me, I do not mean to read —
And they would go and kiss dead Caesar's wounds,
And dip their napkins in his sacred blood,
145   Yea, beg a hair of him for memory,
And, dying, mention it within their wills,
Bequeathing it as a rich legacy
Unto their issue.
FOURTH PLEBEIAN We'll hear the will. Read it, Mark
        Antony.
150   **ALL** The will, the will! We will hear Caesar's will.
ANTONY Have patience, gentle friends, I must not read it.
It is not meet you know how Caesar loved you.
You are not wood, you are not stones, but men:
And being men, hearing the will of Caesar,
155   It will inflame you, it will make you mad;
'Tis good you know not that you are his heirs,
For if you should, O, what would come of it!
FOURTH PLEBEIAN Read the will. We'll hear it, Antony.
You shall read us the will, Caesar's will.
160   **ANTONY** Will you be patient? Will you stay awhile?
I have o'ershot myself to tell you of it.
I fear I wrong the honourable men
Whose daggers have stabbed Caesar: I do fear it.
FOURTH PLEBEIAN They were traitors: honourable men?
165   **ALL** The will, the testament!
SECOND PLEBEIAN They were villains, murderers. The
will, read the will.
ANTONY You will compel me then to read the will:
Then make a ring about the corpse of Caesar,
170   And let me show you him that made the will.
Shall I descend? And will you give me leave?
ALL Come down.
SECOND PLEBEIAN Descend.
THIRD PLEBEIAN You shall have leave.   *Antony comes down*
175   **FOURTH PLEBEIAN** A ring. Stand round.

---

140 closet cabinet   **144 dip . . . blood** i.e. as if Caesar were a martyr   **napkins** handkerchiefs   **148 issue**
children   **152 meet** fit   **161 o'ershot myself** gone further than I intended

FIRST PLEBEIAN Stand from the hearse, stand from the
    body.

SECOND PLEBEIAN Room for Antony, most noble Antony.

ANTONY Nay, press not so upon me. Stand far off.

180 **ALL** Stand back: room, bear back.

ANTONY If you have tears, prepare to shed them now.
    You all do know this mantle. I remember
    The first time ever Caesar put it on.
    'Twas on a summer's evening in his tent,
185   That day he overcame the Nervii.
    Look, in this place ran Cassius' dagger through:
    See what a rent the envious Casca made:
    Through this, the well-belovèd Brutus stabbed,
    And as he plucked his cursèd steel away,
190   Mark how the blood of Caesar followed it,
    As rushing out of doors, to be resolved
    If Brutus so unkindly knocked or no,
    For Brutus, as you know, was Caesar's angel.—
    Judge, O you gods, how dearly Caesar loved him.—
195   This was the most unkindest cut of all.
    For when the noble Caesar saw him stab,
    Ingratitude, more strong than traitors' arms,
    Quite vanquished him: then burst his mighty heart,
    And in his mantle muffling up his face,
200   Even at the base of Pompey's statue —
    Which all the while ran blood — great Caesar fell.
    O, what a fall was there, my countrymen!
    Then I, and you, and all of us fell down,
    Whilst bloody treason flourished over us.
205   O, now you weep, and I perceive you feel
    The dint of pity: these are gracious drops.
    Kind souls, what weep you when you but behold
    Our Caesar's vesture wounded? Look you here,   *Uncovers the body*
    Here is himself, marred as you see with traitors.

210 **FIRST PLEBEIAN** O, piteous spectacle!

SECOND PLEBEIAN O, noble Caesar!

THIRD PLEBEIAN O, woeful day!

FOURTH PLEBEIAN O, traitors, villains!

FIRST PLEBEIAN O, most bloody sight!

---

176 from back from   **hearse** coffin or stand on which the body rests   **179 far** further   **182 mantle**
cloak   **185 Nervii** Belgian tribe of warriors defeated by Caesar   **187 rent** tear, slash   **191 As** as if it were
192 unkindly cruelly/unnaturally   **193 angel** favourite, dearest friend/protective spirit   **204 flourished**
triumphed/prospered/brandished (its sword)   **206 dint** impression, mark   **gracious** virtuous/blessed
208 vesture clothing   **209 marred** spoiled, stained   **with** by

215 **SECOND PLEBEIAN** We will be revenged.
ALL Revenge! About! Seek! Burn! Fire! Kill! Slay!
   Let not a traitor live!
ANTONY Stay, countrymen.
FIRST PLEBEIAN Peace there, hear the noble Antony.
220 **SECOND PLEBEIAN** We'll hear him, we'll follow him, we'll
   die with him.
ANTONY Good friends, sweet friends, let me not stir
      you up
   To such a sudden flood of mutiny:
   They that have done this deed are honourable.
225 What private griefs they have, alas, I know not,
   That made them do it: they are wise and honourable
   And will no doubt with reasons answer you.
   I come not, friends, to steal away your hearts:
   I am no orator, as Brutus is;
230 But as you know me all a plain blunt man
   That love my friend, and that they know full well
   That gave me public leave to speak of him,
   For I have neither wit, nor words, nor worth,
   Action, nor utterance, nor the power of speech,
235 To stir men's blood. I only speak right on:
   I tell you that which you yourselves do know,
   Show you sweet Caesar's wounds, poor poor dumb
      mouths,
   And bid them speak for me. But were I Brutus,
   And Brutus Antony, there were an Antony
240 Would ruffle up your spirits, and put a tongue
   In every wound of Caesar that should move
   The stones of Rome to rise and mutiny.
ALL We'll mutiny.
FIRST PLEBEIAN We'll burn the house of Brutus.
245 **THIRD PLEBEIAN** Away, then, come, seek the
         conspirators.
ANTONY Yet hear me, countrymen, yet hear me speak.
ALL Peace ho, hear Antony, most noble Antony.
ANTONY Why, friends, you go to do you know not what:
   Wherein hath Caesar thus deserved your loves?
250 Alas, you know not. I must tell you then:
   You have forgot the will I told you of.

---

216 **About!** Get moving!   225 **private griefs** personal grievances   229 **orator** eloquent speaker, master of rhetoric   230 **plain blunt** plain-speaking and forthright   233 **wit** intelligence   234 **Action** gestures (used by a skilled orator to reinforce his words)   235 **right on** directly, truthfully   238 **Brutus** i.e. a skilled orator   240 **ruffle up** incite, enrage   249 **Wherein** for what

ALL Most true. The will: let's stay and hear the will.

ANTONY Here is the will, and under Caesar's seal.
      To every Roman citizen he gives,
255   To every several man, seventy-five drachmas.

SECOND PLEBEIAN Most noble Caesar, we'll revenge his
      death.

THIRD PLEBEIAN O royal Caesar.

ANTONY Hear me with patience.

ALL Peace ho.

260 **ANTONY** Moreover, he hath left you all his walks,
      His private arbours and new-planted orchards,
      On this side Tiber. He hath left them you
      And to your heirs for ever: common pleasures
      To walk abroad and recreate yourselves.
265   Here was a Caesar: when comes such another?

FIRST PLEBEIAN Never, never. Come, away, away:
      We'll burn his body in the holy place,
      And with the brands fire the traitors' houses.
      Take up the body.

270 **SECOND PLEBEIAN** Go fetch fire.

THIRD PLEBEIAN Pluck down benches.

FOURTH PLEBEIAN Pluck down forms, windows, any-
      thing.   *Exeunt Plebeians*   **With the body**

ANTONY Now let it work. Mischief, thou art afoot:
275   Take thou what course thou wilt.—
Enter Servant
                                        How now, fellow?

SERVANT Sir, Octavius is already come to Rome.

ANTONY Where is he?

SERVANT He and Lepidus are at Caesar's house.

ANTONY And thither will I straight, to visit him:
280   He comes upon a wish. Fortune is merry
      And in this mood will give us anything.

SERVANT I heard him say Brutus and Cassius
      Are rid like madmen through the gates of Rome.

ANTONY Belike they had some notice of the people
285   How I had moved them. Bring me to Octavius.
                                        Exeunt

---

255 several individual   **drachmas** silver coins; **seventy-five** would be a generous sum   **261 orchards**
gardens   **263 common pleasures** public parks, pleasure gardens   **264 recreate** enjoy   **268 brands**
burning logs   **fire** set fire to   **272 forms** benches   **windows** shutters   **274 Mischief** evil, harm
279 straight (go) straight away   **280 upon a wish** just as I would have wished   **merry** in good spirits,
inclined towards us   **283 Are rid** have ridden   **284 Belike** probably   **notice of** news about

[Act 3 Scene 3]

running scene 7 continues

Enter Cinna the poet, and after him the Plebeians

CINNA I dreamt tonight that I did feast with Caesar,
And things unluckily charge my fantasy:
I have no will to wander forth of doors,
Yet something leads me forth.

5 **FIRST PLEBEIAN** What is your name?

SECOND PLEBEIAN Whither are you going?

THIRD PLEBEIAN Where do you dwell?

FOURTH PLEBEIAN Are you a married man or a bachelor?

SECOND PLEBEIAN Answer every man directly.

10 **FIRST PLEBEIAN** Ay, and briefly.

FOURTH PLEBEIAN Ay, and wisely.

THIRD PLEBEIAN Ay, and truly, you were best.

CINNA What is my name? Whither am I going? Where
do I dwell? Am I a married man or a bachelor? Then,
15 to answer every man directly and briefly, wisely and
truly: wisely I say I am a bachelor.

SECOND PLEBEIAN That's as much as to say they are
fools that marry: you'll bear me a bang for that, I
fear. Proceed, directly.

20 **CINNA** Directly, I am going to Caesar's funeral.

FIRST PLEBEIAN As a friend or an enemy?

CINNA As a friend.

SECOND PLEBEIAN That matter is answered directly.

FOURTH PLEBEIAN For your dwelling, briefly.

25 **CINNA** Briefly, I dwell by the Capitol.

THIRD PLEBEIAN Your name, sir, truly.

CINNA Truly, my name is Cinna.

FIRST PLEBEIAN Tear him to pieces, he's a conspirator.

CINNA I am Cinna the Poet, I am Cinna the Poet.

30 **FOURTH PLEBEIAN** Tear him for his bad verses, tear him
for his bad verses.

CINNA I am not Cinna the conspirator.

FOURTH PLEBEIAN It is no matter, his name's Cinna.
Pluck but his name out of his heart and turn him
35 going.

3.3 *Location: a street in Rome* **1 tonight** last night **2 unluckily ... fantasy** ominously burden my imagination **3 forth** out **9 directly** without evasion/immediately **18 bear ... bang** get a beating **28 he's a conspirator** the First Plebeian confuses Cinna with the conspirator of the same name **34 Pluck** tear, wrench **turn him going** set him on his way

THIRD PLEBEIAN Tear him, tear him! Come, brands, ho!	*They attack*
Fire-brands! To Brutus', to Cassius', burn all! Some	*Cinna*
to Decius' house, and some to Casca's; some to	
Ligarius'! Away, go!	

Exeunt all the Plebeians [dragging Cinna]

Act 4 [Scene 1]   *running scene 8*

Enter Antony, Octavius and Lepidus

ANTONY These many, then, shall die: their names are	*Shows a list*
pricked.	

OCTAVIUS Your brother too must die: consent you,
 Lepidus?
LEPIDUS I do consent.
OCTAVIUS Prick him down, Antony.
5 **LEPIDUS** Upon condition Publius shall not live,
 Who is your sister's son, Mark Antony.
ANTONY He shall not live; look, with a spot I damn
 him.
 But, Lepidus, go you to Caesar's house:
 Fetch the will hither, and we shall determine
10 How to cut off some charge in legacies.
LEPIDUS What, shall I find you here?
OCTAVIUS Or here, or at the Capitol.   *Exit Lepidus*
ANTONY This is a slight unmeritable man,
 Meet to be sent on errands: is it fit,
15 The three-fold world divided, he should stand
 One of the three to share it?
OCTAVIUS So you thought him,
 And took his voice who should be pricked to die
 In our black sentence and proscription.
20 **ANTONY** Octavius, I have seen more days than you,
 And though we lay these honours on this man
 To ease ourselves of divers sland'rous loads,

4.1 *Location: A private place, Rome* **1 pricked** marked down   **2 Your brother** Lucius Aemilius
Paulus, a supporter of Brutus   **7 spot** mark (against his name); may play on the sense of 'moral stain',
which would cause **damn** to resonate with its religious sense   **damn** condemn (legally)   **10 cut . . .**
legacies reduce some of the cost entailed by Caesar's legacies (to the people; the suggestion is that the will is
to be altered)   **12 Or** either   **13 slight** worthless, insignificant   **14 Meet** fit   **15 The . . . divided** after
Caesar's fall, the Roman empire was divided into three parts, each ruled by one of the triumvirs (Octavius,
Antony and Lepidus)   **18 voice** vote (regarding)   **19 black sentence** sentencing of men to death
proscription branding of men as outlaws (which meant their property was confiscated)   **20 have . . . days**
i.e. am older   **22 divers sland'rous loads** various burdensome accusations

He shall but bear them as the ass bears gold,
To groan and sweat under the business,
25   Either led or driven, as we point the way:
And having brought our treasure where we will,
Then take we down his load, and turn him off —
Like to the empty ass — to shake his ears
And graze in commons.
30   **OCTAVIUS** You may do your will:
But he's a tried and valiant soldier.
ANTONY So is my horse, Octavius, and for that
I do appoint him store of provender.
It is a creature that I teach to fight,
35   To wind, to stop, to run directly on,
His corporal motion governed by my spirit,
And, in some taste, is Lepidus but so:
He must be taught, and trained, and bid go forth —
A barren-spirited fellow; one that feeds
40   On objects, arts and imitations
Which, out of use and staled by other men,
Begin his fashion. Do not talk of him
But as a property. And now, Octavius,
Listen great things. Brutus and Cassius
45   Are levying powers. We must straight make head:
Therefore let our alliance be combined,
Our best friends made, our means stretched,
And let us presently go sit in counsel,
How covert matters may be best disclosed,
50   And open perils surest answerèd.
OCTAVIUS Let us do so, for we are at the stake
And bayed about with many enemies,
And some that smile have in their hearts, I fear,
Millions of mischiefs.   *Exeunt*

---

24 **business** task/load   26 **will** want it   27 **off** away   28 **empty** unburdened, idle   29 **commons** public
fields   31 **tried** experienced   33 **appoint...provender** provide him with plenty of food   35 **wind** turn
sharply   36 **corporeal** bodily   37 **taste** degree, sense   39 **barren-spirited** dull-minded, lacking
initiative   40 **objects...imitations** i.e. trivialities, curiosities, things of fashion   41 **staled** worn out, made
stale   42 **Begin his fashion** i.e. he takes as fashionable   43 **property** means to an end   44 **Listen**
hear   45 **levying powers** raising armies   **make head** muster troops   46 **combined** united, of one mind
47 **made** decided (upon), secured   **stretched** extended as far as possible   48 **presently** immediately
sit in counsel i.e. discuss, be advised   49 **covert...disclosed** hidden affairs may best be revealed
50 **open** visible, apparent   **surest** most securely and decisively   51 **at the stake** tied to a stake, like a bear
being baited with dogs   52 **bayed about** surrounded   54 **mischiefs** evils, harms

[Act 4 Scene 2]   *running scene 9*

Drum. Enter Brutus, Lucilius and the army. Titinius and
Pindarus meet them

BRUTUS Stand ho.
LUCILIUS Give the word, ho, and stand.
BRUTUS What now, Lucilius, is Cassius near?
LUCILIUS He is at hand, and Pindarus is come
5   To do you salutation from his master.
BRUTUS He greets me well. Your master, Pindarus,
       In his own change, or by ill officers,
       Hath given me some worthy cause to wish
       Things done, undone: but if he be at hand
10   I shall be satisfied.
PINDARUS I do not doubt
       But that my noble master will appear
       Such as he is, full of regard and honour.
BRUTUS He is not doubted.— A word, Lucilius.   *Brutus and Lucilius*
15   How he received you: let me be resolved.   *speak apart*
LUCILIUS With courtesy and with respect enough,
       But not with such familiar instances,
       Nor with such free and friendly conference
       As he hath used of old.
20 **BRUTUS** Thou hast described
       A hot friend, cooling: ever note, Lucilius,
       When love begins to sicken and decay
       It useth an enforced ceremony.
       There are no tricks in plain and simple faith:
25   But hollow men, like horses hot at hand,
       Make gallant show, and promise of their mettle:
Low march within
       But when they should endure the bloody spur,
       They fall their crests, and like deceitful jades
       Sink in the trial. Comes his army on?

4.2 *Location: a camp near Sardis (the capital of the ancient kingdom of Lydia, Asia Minor); outside Brutus' tent, into which the action then moves*   **1 Stand ho** halt   **2 Give . . . ho** pass on the command (to halt)   **5 his master** i.e. Cassius   **7 change** i.e. changed behaviour, altered attitude   **ill officers** unruly, poor subordinates   **8 worthy** justifiable/substantial   **10 be satisfied** be resolved, have an explanation   **13 regard** respect   **15 he** i.e. Cassius   **resolved** informed   **17 familiar instances** signs of friendship   **18 conference** conversation   **21 hot** eager, devoted   **ever** always   **23 useth . . . ceremony** manifests itself with forced courtesy   **25 hollow** insincere   **hot at hand** eager at the outset   **26 gallant** fine, splendid   **mettle** vigour, spirit   **26 *march*** i.e. march played on drums   **27 bloody** i.e. spattered with blood from the horse's sides   **28 fall** let fall   **crests** necks   **jades** worn-out horses   **29 Sink . . . trial** fail when put to the test

30 **LUCILIUS** They mean this night in Sardis to be quartered:
       The greater part, the horse in general,
       Are come with Cassius.
    Enter Cassius and his powers
    BRUTUS Hark, he is arrived:
       March gently on to meet him.
35 **CASSIUS** Stand ho.
    BRUTUS Stand ho. Speak the word along.
    FIRST SOLDIER Stand.
    SECOND SOLDIER Stand.
    THIRD SOLDIER Stand.
40 **CASSIUS** Most noble brother, you have done me wrong.
    BRUTUS Judge me, you gods; wrong I mine enemies?
       And if not so, how should I wrong a brother?
    CASSIUS Brutus, this sober form of yours hides wrongs,
       And when you do them—
45 **BRUTUS** Cassius, be content.
       Speak your griefs softly. I do know you well:
       Before the eyes of both our armies here —
       Which should perceive nothing but love from us —
       Let us not wrangle. Bid them move away:
50   Then in my tent, Cassius, enlarge your griefs,
       And I will give you audience.
    CASSIUS Pindarus,
       Bid our commanders lead their charges off
       A little from this ground.
55 **BRUTUS** Lucilius, do you the like, and let no man
       Come to our tent till we have done our conference.
       Let Lucius and Titinius guard our door.
                          Exeunt. Brutus and Cassius remain
    CASSIUS That you have wronged me doth appear in this: *They enter*
       You have condemned and noted Lucius Pella   *the tent*
60   For taking bribes here of the Sardians;
       Wherein my letters, praying on his side
       Because I knew the man, was slighted off.
    BRUTUS You wronged yourself to write in such a case.
    CASSIUS In such a time as this it is not meet
65   That every nice offence should bear his comment.

---

30 **quartered** billeted, lodged   31 **horse in general** entire cavalry   32 *powers* troops   34 **gently** nobly/
in an unthreatening manner   40 **brother** brother-in-law   42 **should** i.e. could I possibly   46 **griefs**
grievances   50 **enlarge** give free voice to   51 **give you audience** listen to you   53 **charges** troops   **off**
away   59 **noted** disgraced, discredited   61 **praying** entreating   62 **slighted off** slightingly dismissed
64 **meet** appropriate   65 **nice** petty   **bear his comment** be subject to such criticism

BRUTUS Let me tell you, Cassius, you yourself
　　Are much condemned to have an itching palm,
　　To sell and mart your offices for gold
　　To undeservers.
70　**CASSIUS** I, an itching palm?
　　You know that you are Brutus that speaks this,
　　Or by the gods, this speech were else your last.
　　BRUTUS The name of Cassius honours this corruption,
　　And chastisement doth therefore hide his head.
75　**CASSIUS** Chastisement?
　　BRUTUS Remember March, the Ides of March remember:
　　Did not great Julius bleed for justice' sake?
　　What villain touched his body, that did stab
　　And not for justice? What, shall one of us,
80　That struck the foremost man of all this world
　　But for supporting robbers: shall we now
　　Contaminate our fingers with base bribes?
　　And sell the mighty space of our large honours
　　For so much trash as may be graspèd thus?
85　I had rather be a dog and bay the moon,
　　Than such a Roman.
　　CASSIUS Brutus, bait not me,
　　I'll not endure it: you forget yourself
　　To hedge me in. I am a soldier, I,
90　Older in practice, abler than yourself
　　To make conditions.
　　BRUTUS Go to, you are not Cassius.
　　CASSIUS I am.
　　BRUTUS I say you are not.
95　**CASSIUS** Urge me no more, I shall forget myself.
　　Have mind upon your health: tempt me no further.
　　BRUTUS Away, slight man!
　　CASSIUS Is't possible?
　　BRUTUS Hear me, for I will speak.
100　Must I give way and room to your rash choler?
　　Shall I be frighted when a madman stares?
　　CASSIUS O ye gods, ye gods, must I endure all this?

---

67 condemned . . . palm to blame for your greed　**68 mart** trade, barter　**offices** positions of responsibility　**71 You . . . last** i.e. if you weren't my friend Brutus, I'd kill you for saying this　**73 honours** gives honour to　**74 chastisement** punishment　**hide his head** i.e. is not enforced (with the suggestion of a head hung in shame)　**81 But** merely　**supporting robbers** i.e. permitting corruption　**83 large honours** great reputations/powerful positions　**84 trash** money　**85 bay** howl at　**89 hedge me in** restrict me, challenge my authority　**91 make conditions** manage affairs　**92 Go to** expression of dismissive contempt　**95 forget myself** i.e. lose my temper　**96 Have mind upon** remember, be concerned for　**97 slight** worthless, insignificant/thin, lean　**100 way and room** scope　**choler** rage

BRUTUS All this? Ay, more: fret till your proud heart
    break.
    Go show your slaves how choleric you are,
105   And make your bondmen tremble. Must I budge?
    Must I observe you? Must I stand and crouch
    Under your testy humour? By the gods,
    You shall digest the venom of your spleen
    Though it do split you. For, from this day forth,
110   I'll use you for my mirth, yea, for my laughter,
    When you are waspish.
CASSIUS Is it come to this?
BRUTUS You say you are a better soldier:
    Let it appear so; make your vaunting true
115   And it shall please me well. For mine own part,
    I shall be glad to learn of noble men.
CASSIUS You wrong me every way: you wrong me,
    Brutus.
    I said, an elder soldier, not a better.
    Did I say 'better'?
120 **BRUTUS** If you did, I care not.
CASSIUS When Caesar lived, he durst not thus have
    moved me.
BRUTUS Peace, peace, you durst not so have tempted
    him.
CASSIUS I durst not?
BRUTUS No.
125 **CASSIUS** What? Durst not tempt him?
BRUTUS For your life you durst not.
CASSIUS Do not presume too much upon my love:
    I may do that I shall be sorry for.
BRUTUS You have done that you should be sorry for.
130   There is no terror, Cassius, in your threats,
    For I am armed so strong in honesty
    That they pass by me as the idle wind,
    Which I respect not. I did send to you
    For certain sums of gold, which you denied me,
135   For I can raise no money by vile means:
    By heaven, I had rather coin my heart

---

105 budge flinch/give way　**106 observe** honour, wait upon　**crouch** cringe　**107 testy humour**
irritable mood　**108 digest** i.e. be obliged to swallow　**spleen** bad temper, anger (the spleen was thought to
be the seat of strong emotions)　**114 vaunting** boasting　**116 of** from/about　**121 durst . . . me** would not
have dared provoke me is such a manner　**127 presume** rely　**132 idle** useless/frivolous/inactive
135 vile means shameful methods (i.e. corruption, extortion)　**136 coin** turn into money

And drop my blood for drachmas, than to wring
From the hard hands of peasants their vile trash
By any indirection. I did send
140 To you for gold to pay my legions,
Which you denied me: was that done like Cassius?
Should I have answered Caius Cassius so?
When Marcus Brutus grows so covetous,
To lock such rascal counters from his friends,
145 Be ready, gods, with all your thunderbolts,
Dash him to pieces!

CASSIUS I denied you not.

BRUTUS You did.

CASSIUS I did not. He was but a fool that brought
150 My answer back. Brutus hath rived my heart:
A friend should bear his friend's infirmities;
But Brutus makes mine greater than they are.

BRUTUS I do not, till you practise them on me.

CASSIUS You love me not.

155 BRUTUS I do not like your faults.

CASSIUS A friendly eye could never see such faults.

BRUTUS A flatterer's would not, though they do appear
As huge as high Olympus.

CASSIUS Come, Antony, and young Octavius, come,
160 Revenge yourselves alone on Cassius,
For Cassius is aweary of the world:
Hated by one he loves, braved by his brother,
Checked like a bondman, all his faults observed,
Set in a notebook, learned and conned by rote
165 To cast into my teeth. O, I could weep
My spirit from mine eyes! There is my dagger,
And here my naked breast: within, a heart
Dearer than Pluto's mine, richer than gold.
If that thou be'st a Roman, take it forth.
170 I that denied thee gold will give my heart:
Strike as thou didst at Caesar, for I know,
When thou didst hate him worst, thou lov'dst him
    better
Than ever thou lov'dst Cassius.

---

137 drop shed   drachmas silver coins   138 hard toughened with work/ungenerous   vile worthless,
lowly, contemptible   139 indirection deceit, dishonesty   144 rascal counters worthless coins   150 rived
split   151 infirmities flaws, weaknesses   162 braved challenged, defied   163 Checked rebuked/
restrained   164 conned by rote memorized through repetition   168 Dearer more valuable   Pluto
fabulously rich Greek god of the underworld   mine silver and gold mines   169 take it forth i.e. tear this
heart out

BRUTUS Sheathe your dagger.
175   Be angry when you will, it shall have scope:
           Do what you will, dishonour shall be humour.
           O Cassius, you are yokèd with a lamb
           That carries anger as the flint bears fire,
           Who, much enforcèd, shows a hasty spark
180   And straight is cold again.
CASSIUS   Hath Cassius lived
           To be but mirth and laughter to his Brutus,
           When grief and blood ill-tempered vexeth him?
BRUTUS When I spoke that, I was ill-tempered too.
185 **CASSIUS** Do you confess so much? Give me your hand.
BRUTUS And my heart too.   *They embrace*
CASSIUS O Brutus!
BRUTUS What's the matter?
CASSIUS Have not you love enough to bear with me,
190   When that rash humour which my mother gave me
           Makes me forgetful?
BRUTUS   Yes, Cassius, and from henceforth
           When you are over-earnest with your Brutus,
           He'll think your mother chides, and leave you so.
           Enter a Poet [with Lucilius and Titinius]
195 **POET** Let me go in to see the generals.
           There is some grudge between 'em, 'tis not meet
           They be alone.
LUCILIUS You shall not come to them.
POET Nothing but death shall stay me.
200 **CASSIUS** How now? What's the matter?
POET For shame, you generals; what do you mean?
           Love and be friends, as two such men should be,
           For I have seen more years, I'm sure, than ye.
CASSIUS Ha, ha, how vilely doth this cynic rhyme!
205 **BRUTUS** Get you hence, sirrah. Saucy fellow, hence.
CASSIUS Bear with him, Brutus, 'tis his fashion.

---

176 **dishonour . . . humour** i.e. your dishonourable behaviour shall be attributed to a bad mood   177 **lamb** i.e. the supposedly gentle Brutus   179 **enforcèd** acted upon by force (i.e. struck to create a spark)   **hasty** quick, brief   183 **blood ill-tempered** a disordered temperament (physical and mental health was thought to be governed by the four bodily fluids or 'humours'; the excess of one would lead to illness or an imbalanced mood)   190 **rash humour** i.e. choler, the humour responsible for impetuous anger   191 **forgetful** irrational, badly behaved   194 **leave you so** i.e. leave it at that   201 **mean** i.e. think you are doing   204 **cynic** i.e. fault-finder (literally, a follower of Cynic philosophy, which disdained pleasure and enjoyment)   205 **Saucy** insolent   206 **fashion** manner

BRUTUS I'll know his humour when he knows his time:
What should the wars do with these jigging fools?
Companion, hence.

210 **CASSIUS** Away, away, be gone.   *Exit Poet*

BRUTUS Lucilius and Titinius, bid the commanders
Prepare to lodge their companies tonight.

CASSIUS And come yourselves, and bring Messala
with you
Immediately to us.   [*Exeunt Lucilius and Titinius*]

215 **BRUTUS** Lucius, a bowl of wine.   *Calls*

CASSIUS I did not think you could have been so angry.

BRUTUS O Cassius, I am sick of many griefs.

CASSIUS Of your philosophy you make no use,
If you give place to accidental evils.

220 **BRUTUS** No man bears sorrow better. Portia is dead.

CASSIUS Ha? Portia?

BRUTUS She is dead.

CASSIUS How scaped I killing when I crossed you so?
O, insupportable and touching loss!

225 Upon what sickness?

BRUTUS Impatient of my absence,
And grief that young Octavius with Mark Antony
Have made themselves so strong — for with her
death
That tidings came — with this she fell distract,

230 And — her attendants absent — swallowed fire.

CASSIUS And died so?

BRUTUS Even so.

CASSIUS O ye immortal gods!

Enter Boy [*Lucius*] *with wine and tapers*

BRUTUS Speak no more of her. Give me a bowl of wine.

235 In this I bury all unkindness, Cassius.   *Drinks*

CASSIUS My heart is thirsty for that noble pledge.
Fill, Lucius, till the wine o'erswell the cup: *Drinks*
I cannot drink too much of Brutus' love.
                                        [*Exit Lucius*]

Enter Titinius and Messala

---

207 I'll ... time I'll acknowledge his manner when he recognizes the proper occasion for it (**time** plays on the sense of 'musical time, rhythm')   **208 jigging** rhyming in a jerking and metrically unsophisticated manner   **209 Companion** rogue, rascal   **217 of** with   **218 philosophy** usually identified as Stoicism, which valued endurance in the face of hardship, but according to Plutarch, Brutus was a Platonist   **219 place** room/precedence   **accidental evils** chance misfortunes   **223 scaped** escaped   **crossed** challenged, opposed   **224 touching** deeply felt   **225 Upon** as a result of   **228 her** i.e. news of her   **229 That tidings** i.e. news of Octavius and Antony's power   **distract** mad, deranged   **230 fire** specifically, burning coals   **237 o'erswell** overflow

BRUTUS Come in, Titinius. Welcome, good Messala.
240   Now sit we close about this taper here
    And call in question our necessities.   *They sit*
CASSIUS Portia, art thou gone?
BRUTUS No more, I pray you.—
    Messala, I have here receivèd letters,   *Shows letters*
245   That young Octavius and Mark Antony
    Come down upon us with a mighty power,
    Bending their expedition toward Philippi.
MESSALA Myself have letters of the selfsame tenor.
BRUTUS With what addition?
250   **MESSALA** That by proscription and bills of outlawry,
    Octavius, Antony and Lepidus
    Have put to death an hundred senators.
BRUTUS Therein our letters do not well agree:
    Mine speak of seventy senators that died
255   By their proscriptions, Cicero being one.
CASSIUS Cicero one?
MESSALA Cicero is dead,
    And by that order of proscription.
    Had you your letters from your wife, my lord?
260   **BRUTUS** No, Messala.
MESSALA Nor nothing in your letters writ of her?
BRUTUS Nothing, Messala.
MESSALA That, methinks, is strange.
BRUTUS Why ask you? Hear you aught of her in yours?
265   **MESSALA** No, my lord.
BRUTUS Now, as you are a Roman, tell me true.
MESSALA Then like a Roman bear the truth I tell,
    For certain she is dead, and by strange manner.
BRUTUS Why, farewell, Portia: we must die, Messala:
270   With meditating that she must die once,
    I have the patience to endure it now.
MESSALA Even so great men great losses should endure.
CASSIUS I have as much of this in art as you,
    But yet my nature could not bear it so.
275   **BRUTUS** Well, to our work alive. What do you think
    Of marching to Philippi presently?

---

241 **call in question** discuss   247 **Bending** directing   **expedition** speedy setting forth/military enterprise   **Philippi** city in Macedonia   248 **tenor** drift, substance   250 **proscription . . . outlawry** i.e. legislation declaring some people to be outlaws punishable by death   270 **must die once** had to die some day   272 **Even so** in just such a manner   273 **art** practised fortitude, learned behaviour   274 **nature** natural feelings   **bear it** carry it off, maintain it   275 **alive** concerning those who are living/of present importance

CASSIUS I do not think it good.

BRUTUS Your reason?

CASSIUS This it is:

280 'Tis better that the enemy seek us,
So shall he waste his means, weary his soldiers,
Doing himself offence, whilst we, lying still,
Are full of rest, defence and nimbleness.

BRUTUS Good reasons must of force give place to better:

285 The people 'twixt Philippi and this ground
Do stand but in a forced affection,
For they have grudged us contribution.
The enemy, marching along by them,
By them shall make a fuller number up,

290 Come on refreshed, new-added and encouraged,
From which advantage shall we cut him off
If at Philippi we do face him there,
These people at our back.

CASSIUS Hear me, good brother.

295 **BRUTUS** Under your pardon. You must note beside
That we have tried the utmost of our friends,
Our legions are brim-full, our cause is ripe.
The enemy increaseth every day:
We, at the height, are ready to decline.

300 There is a tide in the affairs of men
Which, taken at the flood, leads on to fortune:
Omitted, all the voyage of their life
Is bound in shallows and in miseries.
On such a full sea are we now afloat,

305 And we must take the current when it serves,
Or lose our ventures.

CASSIUS Then with your will go on:
We'll along ourselves, and meet them at Philippi.

BRUTUS The deep of night is crept upon our talk,

310 And nature must obey necessity,
Which we will niggard with a little rest.
There is no more to say.

---

282 **offence** damage/attack (the opposite of **defence**)   284 **force** necessity   **place** way   286 **affection**
allegiance   287 **contribution** resources, supplies (including soldiers)   289 **make ... up** increase its
numbers   290 **new-added** reinforced, with augmented numbers   293 **These ... back** behind us
(supporting us/cut off from our enemy)   295 **Under your pardon** i.e. allow me to continue   296 **tried** put
(successfully) to the test   301 **taken ... flood** i.e. set sail on when it is in   302 **Omitted** neglected
303 **bound in shallows** confined to shallow waters   306 **ventures** investments at sea/enterprises
308 **along** go along   311 **niggard** fob off, stint

CASSIUS No more. Goodnight.
    Early tomorrow will we rise, and hence.
Enter Lucius
315 **BRUTUS** Lucius. My gown.—   [*Exit Lucius*]
                    Farewell, good Messala.—
    Goodnight, Titinius.— Noble, noble Cassius,
    Goodnight, and good repose.
CASSIUS O my dear brother,
    This was an ill beginning of the night:
320 Never come such division 'tween our souls.
    Let it not, Brutus.
Enter Lucius with the gown
BRUTUS Everything is well.
CASSIUS Goodnight, my lord.
BRUTUS Goodnight, good brother.
325 **TITINIUS** *and* **MESSALA** Goodnight, Lord Brutus.
BRUTUS Farewell, every one.
                Exeunt [*Cassius, Titinius and Messala*]
    Give me the gown. Where is thy instrument?
LUCIUS Here in the tent.
BRUTUS What, thou speak'st drowsily?
330 Poor knave, I blame thee not: thou art o'er-watched.
    Call Claudio and some other of my men.
    I'll have them sleep on cushions in my tent.
LUCIUS Varrus and Claudio!   *Calls*
Enter Varrus and Claudio
VARRUS Calls my lord?
335 **BRUTUS** I pray you, sirs, lie in my tent and sleep.
    It may be I shall raise you by and by
    On business to my brother Cassius.
VARRUS So please you, we will stand and watch your
    pleasure.
BRUTUS I will not have it so: lie down, good sirs,
340 It may be I shall otherwise bethink me.   *They lie down*
    Look, Lucius, here's the book I sought for so:
    I put it in the pocket of my gown.
LUCIUS I was sure your lordship did not give it me.
BRUTUS Bear with me, good boy, I am much forgetful.
345 Canst thou hold up thy heavy eyes awhile
    And touch thy instrument a strain or two?

---

315 **gown** dressing-gown   327 **instrument** musical instrument, perhaps a lute   330 **art o'er-watched** have been awake (perhaps on guard) for too long   336 **raise** rouse, wake   338 **watch your pleasure** remain awake and ready to respond to your needs   340 **otherwise bethink me** i.e. change my mind   346 **touch** i.e. play on

LUCIUS Ay, my lord, an't please you.

BRUTUS It does, my boy.
I trouble thee too much, but thou art willing.

350 **LUCIUS** It is my duty, sir.

BRUTUS I should not urge thy duty past thy might.
I know young bloods look for a time of rest.

LUCIUS I have slept, my lord, already.

BRUTUS It was well done, and thou shalt sleep again.

355 I will not hold thee long. If I do live,
I will be good to thee.

Music, and a song   *Lucius falls asleep*

This is a sleepy tune:— O murderous slumber!
Lay'st thou thy leaden mace upon my boy,
That plays thee music?— Gentle knave, goodnight.

360 I will not do thee so much wrong to wake thee:
If thou dost nod, thou break'st thy instrument,
I'll take it from thee. And, good boy, goodnight.   *Takes away the*
Let me see, let me see; is not the leaf turned down   *instrument*
Where I left reading? Here it is, I think.   *and reads*

Enter the Ghost of Caesar

365 How ill this taper burns. Ha? Who comes here?
I think it is the weakness of mine eyes
That shapes this monstrous apparition.
It comes upon me: art thou any thing?
Art thou some god, some angel, or some devil,

370 That mak'st my blood cold, and my hair to stare?
Speak to me what thou art.

GHOST Thy evil spirit, Brutus.

BRUTUS Why comest thou?

GHOST To tell thee thou shalt see me at Philippi.

375 **BRUTUS** Well: then I shall see thee again?

GHOST Ay, at Philippi.

BRUTUS Why, I will see thee at Philippi, then.

                              [*Exit Ghost*]

Now I have taken heart, thou vanishest.
Ill spirit, I would hold more talk with thee.—

380 Boy, Lucius, Varrus, Claudio! Sirs, awake! Claudio!

LUCIUS The strings, my lord, are false.

BRUTUS He thinks he still is at his instrument.—
Lucius, awake!

---

347 an't if it   **351 might** capabilities, strength   **352 look for** need, expect   **355 hold** detain
357 murderous i.e. that gives the appearance of death   **358 leaden mace** heavy staff of office (used by a
sergeant to arrest offenders by touching them with his mace)   **367 shapes** creates, forms   **monstrous**
unnatural   **370 stare** stand on end   **378 taken heart** gathered my courage   **381 false** out of tune

LUCIUS My lord?
385   BRUTUS Didst thou dream, Lucius, that thou so cried'st
out?
LUCIUS My lord, I do not know that I did cry.
BRUTUS Yes, that thou didst: didst thou see anything?
LUCIUS Nothing, my lord.
BRUTUS Sleep again, Lucius. Sirrah Claudio,
390   Fellow thou, awake!   *To Varrus*
VARRUS My lord?
CLAUDIO My lord?
BRUTUS Why did you so cry out, sirs, in your sleep?
BOTH Did we, my lord?   *They get up*
395   BRUTUS Ay: saw you anything?
VARRUS No, my lord, I saw nothing.
CLAUDIO Nor I, my lord.
BRUTUS Go and commend me to my brother Cassius:
Bid him set on his powers betimes before
400   And we will follow.
BOTH It shall be done, my lord.   *Exeunt*

Act 5 [Scene 1]   *running scene 10*

Enter Octavius, Antony and their army

OCTAVIUS Now, Antony, our hopes are answerèd.
You said the enemy would not come down,
But keep the hills and upper regions:
It proves not so: their battles are at hand.
5   They mean to warn us at Philippi here,
Answering before we do demand of them.
ANTONY Tut, I am in their bosoms, and I know
Wherefore they do it: they could be content
To visit other places, and come down
10   With fearful bravery, thinking by this face
To fasten in our thoughts that they have courage;
But 'tis not so.
Enter a Messenger

---

390 **Fellow thou** thou, fellow   398 **commend me** convey my greetings   399 **set … before** set off with
his troops early in the morning   5.1 *Location: near Philippi*   3 **keep** keep to   4 **battles** battalions
5 **warn** challenge   6 **Answering** responding to/encountering for a fight   **demand of** ask   7 **am …
bosoms** know their secrets   8 **could be content** would like   9 **visit other places** be elsewhere, take up
different positions   **come down** attack (by surprise)   10 **fearful bravery** alarming bravery/a false show of
bravery to hide their fear   **face** show   11 **fasten** fix the impression   12 **'tis not so** they are unable to do
so/they have no courage

MESSENGER Prepare you, generals.
    The enemy comes on in gallant show:
15   Their bloody sign of battle is hung out,
    And something to be done immediately.
ANTONY Octavius, lead your battle softly on,
    Upon the left hand of the even field.
OCTAVIUS Upon the right hand I: keep thou the left.
20 **ANTONY** Why do you cross me in this exigent?
OCTAVIUS I do not cross you: but I will do so.   *March*
Drum. Enter Brutus, Cassius and their army [*Lucilius,*
Titinius, Messala and others]
BRUTUS They stand, and would have parley.
CASSIUS Stand fast, Titinius, we must out and talk.
OCTAVIUS Mark Antony, shall we give sign of battle?
25 **ANTONY** No, Caesar, we will answer on their charge.
    Make forth, the generals would have some words.
OCTAVIUS Stir not until the signal.   *To his officers*
BRUTUS Words before blows: is it so, countrymen? *The armies advance*
OCTAVIUS Not that we love words better, as you do. *towards each other*
30 **BRUTUS** Good words are better than bad strokes,
    Octavius.
ANTONY In your bad strokes, Brutus, you give good
    words:
    Witness the hole you made in Caesar's heart,
    Crying 'Long live! Hail, Caesar!'
CASSIUS Antony,
35   The posture of your blows are yet unknown
    But for your words, they rob the Hybla bees,
    And leave them honeyless.
ANTONY Not stingless too?
BRUTUS O yes, and soundless too,
40   For you have stol'n their buzzing, Antony,
    And very wisely threat before you sting.
ANTONY Villains, you did not so, when your vile daggers
    Hacked one another in the sides of Caesar:
    You showed your teeth like apes, and fawned like
    hounds,

---

14 gallant splendid, smart **15 bloody**...**battle** red flag, a signal for battle **16 to** is to, must **17 softly**
slowly, warily **18 even** level, flat **20 exigent** critical moment **22 have parley** negotiation, during
which hostilities were suspended **25 answer**...**charge** respond when they attack **26 Make forth** go
forward **30 strokes** blows **35 The**...**blows** the nature of your blows, how you will strike **36 for** as
for **your words** refers to Antony's deceptively friendly words to the conspirators after Caesar's murder, or
perhaps to his flattering words to the people regarding Caesar's love for them **Hybla** town in Sicily, famed
for its honey **40 buzzing** plays on the sense of 'rumour-mongering' **41 threat** threaten **42 so** i.e. give
warning **44 showed your teeth** grinned **apes** i.e. fools

45　　　And bowed like bondmen, kissing Caesar's feet;
　　　　Whilst damnèd Casca, like a cur, behind
　　　　Struck Caesar on the neck. O you flatterers!
　　CASSIUS Flatterers? Now, Brutus, thank yourself.
　　　　This tongue had not offended so today
50　　　If Cassius might have ruled.
　　OCTAVIUS Come, come, the cause. If arguing make us
　　　　　　sweat,
　　　　The proof of it will turn to redder drops:
　　　　Look, I draw a sword against conspirators.　　　　　　　　*Draws*
　　　　When think you that the sword goes up again?
55　　　Never, till Caesar's three and thirty wounds
　　　　Be well avenged, or till another Caesar
　　　　Have added slaughter to the sword of traitors.
　　BRUTUS Caesar, thou canst not die by traitors' hands
　　　　Unless thou bring'st them with thee.
60　　**OCTAVIUS** So I hope:
　　　　I was not born to die on Brutus' sword.
　　BRUTUS O, if thou wert the noblest of thy strain,
　　　　Young man, thou couldst not die more honourable.
　　CASSIUS A peevish schoolboy, worthless of such honour,
65　　　Joined with a masquer and a reveller.
　　ANTONY Old Cassius still.
　　OCTAVIUS Come, Antony, away.
　　　　Defiance, traitors, hurl we in your teeth.
　　　　If you dare fight today, come to the field;
70　　　If not, when you have stomachs.
　　　　　　　　　　　Exeunt Octavius, Antony and army
　　CASSIUS Why now, blow wind, swell billow and swim
　　　　　　bark:
　　　　The storm is up and all is on the hazard.
　　BRUTUS Ho, Lucilius, hark, a word with you.
　　Lucilius and Messala stand forth
　　LUCILIUS My lord.　　　　　　　　*Brutus and Lucilius speak apart*
75　　**CASSIUS** Messala.
　　MESSALA What says my general?

---

46 cur dog　**49 This…ruled** i.e. if Cassius had had his way, Antony would have been killed along with Caesar　**51 cause** grounds for hostility, central issue　**52 proof** trial (on the battlefield)　**54 goes up** is sheathed　**56 another Caesar** i.e. myself, Octavius Caesar　**57 added slaughter to** i.e. been killed by **59 thou…thee** i.e. those hands are your own　**62 if** even if　**strain** family line　**63 more honourable** more honourably (than being killed by Brutus)　**64 peevish** foolish/obstinate/ill-tempered　**65 masquer** one who participates in masques (theatrical entertainments involving elaborate costumes and dancing) **70 stomachs** courage, appetites (for battle)　**71 billow** wave　**bark** ship　**72 on the hazard** at stake

CASSIUS Messala,
    This is my birthday: as this very day
    Was Cassius born. Give me thy hand, Messala:
80   Be thou my witness that against my will —
    As Pompey was — am I compelled to set
    Upon one battle all our liberties.
    You know that I held Epicurus strong
    And his opinion: now I change my mind
85   And partly credit things that do presage.
    Coming from Sardis, on our former ensign
    Two mighty eagles fell, and there they perched,
    Gorging and feeding from our soldiers' hands,
    Who to Philippi here consorted us:
90   This morning are they fled away and gone,
    And in their steads do ravens, crows and kites
    Fly o'er our heads and downward look on us
    As we were sickly prey; their shadows seem
    A canopy most fatal, under which
95   Our army lies, ready to give up the ghost.
MESSALA Believe not so.
CASSIUS I but believe it partly,
    For I am fresh of spirit and resolved
    To meet all perils very constantly.
100 BRUTUS Even so, Lucilius.   *To Cassius*
CASSIUS Now, most noble Brutus,
    The gods today stand friendly, that we may,
    Lovers in peace, lead on our days to age.
    But since the affairs of men rests still incertain,
105   Let's reason with the worst that may befall.
    If we do lose this battle, then is this
    The very last time we shall speak together:
    What are you then determinèd to do?
BRUTUS Even by the rule of that philosophy
110   By which I did blame Cato for the death
    Which he did give himself — I know not how,

---

78 as this this   **81 Pompey was** Pompey was reluctantly persuaded into a disastrous final battle with Caesar at Pharsalus in 48 BC   **set** stake   **83 Epicurus** Greek philosopher who believed that the gods were indifferent to human affairs, and thus that omens did not influence the course of events   **85 credit** give credit to, believe   **presage** foretell events   **86 former ensign** foremost military banner   **87 fell** swooped   **89 consorted** accompanied   **91 steads** places   **ravens . . . kites** scavenging birds considered to be bad omens   **93 As** as if   **94 fatal** ominous, boding death   **99 constantly** resolutely   **100 Even so, Lucilius** Brutus finishes his private conversation with Lucilius   **102 The** may the   **103 Lovers** dear friends   **104 rests still** remain always   **105 reason with** consider   **109 philosophy** the anti-suicide sentiment Brutus expresses is Stoic   **110 Cato** Portia's father, an ally of Pompey who committed suicide rather than surrender to Caesar   **111 how** i.e. why

But I do find it cowardly and vile,
For fear of what might fall, so to prevent
The time of life — arming myself with patience
115   To stay the providence of some high powers
That govern us below.
CASSIUS Then, if we lose this battle,
You are contented to be led in triumph
Through the streets of Rome?
120   **BRUTUS** No, Cassius, no: think not, thou noble Roman,
That ever Brutus will go bound to Rome.
He bears too great a mind. But this same day
Must end that work the Ides of March begun.
And whether we shall meet again I know not:
125   Therefore our everlasting farewell take.
For ever and for ever farewell, Cassius.
If we do meet again, why, we shall smile;
If not, why then, this parting was well made.
CASSIUS For ever and for ever farewell, Brutus:
130   If we do meet again, we'll smile indeed;
If not, 'tis true this parting was well made.
BRUTUS Why, then, lead on. O, that a man might know
The end of this day's business ere it come:
But it sufficeth that the day will end,
135   And then the end is known. Come ho, away!

Exeunt

[Act 5 Scene 2]   *running scene 10 continues*

Alarum. Enter Brutus and Messala

BRUTUS Ride, ride, Messala, ride, and give these bills   *Gives orders*
Unto the legions on the other side.
Loud alarum
Let them set on at once, for I perceive
But cold demeanour in Octavio's wing,
5   And sudden push gives them the overthrow.
Ride, ride, Messala: let them all come down.

Exeunt

---

113 fall happen   **prevent**...**life** cut short one's natural lifespan   **115 stay** await   **118 in triumph**
chained to the victor's chariot during the triumphal return to Rome   **122 great** noble   **5.2** *Location: the*
battlefield near Philippi   **0 *Alarum*** call to arms, usually with trumpet or drum   **1 bills** written
commands   **2 other side** i.e. Cassius' division of the army, located in another part of the battlefield   **3 set**
on advance   **4 cold** unenthusiastic/miserable   **Octavio's** i.e. Octavius'   **wing** division of the army
5 push attack   **6 come down** attack (by surprise)

[Act 5 Scene 3]   *running scene 10 continues*

Alarums. Enter Cassius and Titinius

CASSIUS O, look, Titinius, look, the villains fly:
    Myself have to mine own turned enemy:
    This ensign here of mine was turning back.
    I slew the coward, and did take it from him.
5   TITINIUS O Cassius, Brutus gave the word too early,
    Who having some advantage on Octavius,
    Took it too eagerly: his soldiers fell to spoil,
    Whilst we by Antony are all enclosed.
Enter Pindarus
PINDARUS Fly further off, my lord, fly further off.
10   Mark Antony is in your tents, my lord:
    Fly, therefore, noble Cassius, fly far off.
CASSIUS This hill is far enough. Look, look, Titinius:
    Are those my tents where I perceive the fire?
TITINIUS They are, my lord.
15   CASSIUS Titinius, if thou lovest me,
    Mount thou my horse, and hide thy spurs in him,
    Till he have brought thee up to yonder troops
    And here again, that I may rest assured
    Whether yond troops are friend or enemy.
20   TITINIUS I will be here again, even with a thought.
                                  Exit
CASSIUS Go, Pindarus, get higher on that hill:
    My sight was ever thick. Regard Titinius,
    And tell me what thou not'st about the field.   *Pindarus goes aloft*
    This day I breathèd first. Time is come round,
25   And where I did begin, there shall I end.
    My life is run his compass.— Sirrah, what news?
PINDARUS O, my lord!   *Above*
CASSIUS What news?
PINDARUS Titinius is enclosèd round about
30   With horsemen, that make to him on the spur,
    Yet he spurs on. Now they are almost on him:
    Now, Titinius. Now some light: O, he lights too.
    He's ta'en. And, hark, they shout for joy.   *Shout*

5.3   **1 the villains** i.e. Cassius' own troops   **2 mine own** i.e. my own men   **3 ensign** military flag-bearer
4 it i.e. the flag or banner   **7 fell to spoil** were slaughtered   **8 enclosed** surrounded   **16 hide** i.e. dig
hard   **18 here** back here   **20 even with** i.e. as quick as   **22 thick** dim, poor   **Regard** watch   **23 *goes
aloft*** i.e. exits and mounts to the upper staging level or gallery   **24 This . . . first** i.e. it is my birthday
26 is . . . compass has come full circle   **30 on the spur** rapidly   **32 light** alight, dismount   **33 ta'en**
captured

CASSIUS Come down, behold no more.   *Pindarus comes down*

35   O, coward that I am, to live so long,

     To see my best friend ta'en before my face.

Enter Pindarus

     Come hither, sirrah.

     In Parthia did I take thee prisoner,

     And then I swore thee, saving of thy life,

40   That whatsoever I did bid thee do,

     Thou shouldst attempt it. Come now, keep thine
         oath:

     Now be a freeman, and with this good sword

     That ran through Caesar's bowels, search this bosom.

     Stand not to answer: here, take thou the hilts,   *Pindarus takes*

45   And when my face is covered, as 'tis now,   *the sword*

     Guide thou the sword.— Caesar, thou art revenged,   *Covers his face*

     Even with the sword that killed thee.   *Pindarus kills him*

PINDARUS So, I am free, yet would not so have been

     Durst I have done my will. O Cassius,

50   Far from this country Pindarus shall run,

     Where never Roman shall take note of him.   [*Exit*]

Enter Titinius and Messala   *Titinius wears a laurel wreath*

MESSALA It is but change, Titinius, for Octavius

     Is overthrown by noble Brutus' power,

     As Cassius' legions are by Antony.

55 **TITINIUS** These tidings will well comfort Cassius.

MESSALA Where did you leave him?

TITINIUS All disconsolate,

     With Pindarus his bondman, on this hill.

MESSALA Is not that he that lies upon the ground?

60 **TITINIUS** He lies not like the living. O my heart!

MESSALA Is not that he?

TITINIUS No, this was he, Messala,

     But Cassius is no more.— O setting sun:

     As in thy red rays thou dost sink tonight,

65   So in his red blood Cassius' day is set.—

     The sun of Rome is set. Our day is gone:

     Clouds, dews and dangers come: our deeds are done.

     Mistrust of my success hath done this deed.

---

38 Parthia now northern Iran   **39 swore thee** made you swear   **43 bowels** guts, intestines   **search** probe, i.e. stab   **44 Stand** wait   **hilts** sword handle   **48 would ... will** had I been able to act as I wished, I would not have gained freedom in such a manner   **51 take note of** i.e. find   **52 change** exchange of advantages   **55 comfort** hearten, encourage   **67 dews** disease-ridden dampness   **68 Mistrust** Cassius' doubt

MESSALA Mistrust of good success hath done this
    deed.—
70 O hateful error, melancholy's child,
    Why dost thou show to the apt thoughts of men
    The things that are not? O error soon conceived,
    Thou never com'st unto a happy birth
    But kill'st the mother that engendered thee.
75 **TITINIUS** What, Pindarus? Where art thou, Pindarus?
MESSALA Seek him, Titinius, whilst I go to meet
    The noble Brutus, thrusting this report
    Into his ears. I may say, thrusting it:
    For piercing steel and darts envenomèd
80 Shall be as welcome to the ears of Brutus
    As tidings of this sight.
TITINIUS Hie you, Messala,
    And I will seek for Pindarus the while.—
                            [Exit Messala]
    Why didst thou send me forth, brave Cassius?
85 Did I not meet thy friends? And did not they
    Put on my brows this wreath of victory
    And bid me give it thee? Didst thou not hear their
        shouts?
    Alas, thou hast misconstrued everything.
    But hold thee, take this garland on thy brow: *Puts wreath on him*
90 Thy Brutus bid me give it thee, and I
    Will do his bidding.— Brutus, come apace,
    And see how I regarded Caius Cassius.—
    By your leave, gods: this is a Roman's part.—
    Come, Cassius' sword, and find Titinius' heart. *Dies*   *Stabs himself*
    Alarum. Enter Brutus, Messala, Young Cato, Strato,
    Volumnius and Lucilius
95 **BRUTUS** Where, where, Messala, doth his body lie?
MESSALA Lo, yonder, and Titinius mourning it.
BRUTUS Titinius' face is upward.
CATO He is slain.
BRUTUS O Julius Caesar, thou art mighty yet,
100 Thy spirit walks abroad and turns our swords
    In our own proper entrails.   *Low alarums*
CATO Brave Titinius,
    Look whe'er he have not crowned dead Cassius.

---

71 apt readily believing   **72 The...not?** i.e. the apparent capture of Titinius   **74 the mother** i.e. the
melancholy mind   **79 darts** arrows/spears   **envenomèd** poisoned   **86 wreath of victory** i.e. laurel
wreath   **91 apace** quickly   **92 regarded** respected, esteemed   **93 part** role, duty/proper conduct
101 own proper very own   **Low** muted, quiet   **103 whe'er** whether

BRUTUS Are yet two Romans living such as these?—
105   The last of all the Romans, fare thee well:
           It is impossible that ever Rome
           Should breed thy fellow.— Friends, I owe more tears
           To this dead man than you shall see me pay.—
           I shall find time, Cassius: I shall find time.—
110   Come therefore, and to Thasos send his body.
           His funerals shall not be in our camp,
           Lest it discomfort us.— Lucilius, come,
           And come, young Cato: let us to the field.
           Labio and Flavius set our battles on:
115   'Tis three o'clock, and, Romans, yet ere night
           We shall try fortune in a second fight.   *Exeunt*   **With the bodies**

[Act 5 Scene 4]   *running scene 10 continues*

*Alarum. Enter Brutus, Messala, [Young] Cato, Lucilius and
Flavius*

BRUTUS Yet, countrymen: O yet, hold up your heads!
                [Exit, fighting, followed by Messala and Flavius]
CATO What bastard doth not? Who will go with me?
        I will proclaim my name about the field.
        I am the son of Marcus Cato, ho!
5   A foe to tyrants, and my country's friend.
        I am the son of Marcus Cato, ho!
Enter soldiers and fight
LUCILIUS And I am Brutus, Marcus Brutus, I!
        Brutus, my country's friend: know me for Brutus!   **Young Cato falls**
        O young and noble Cato, art thou down?
10   Why, now thou diest as bravely as Titinius,
        And mayst be honoured, being Cato's son.
FIRST SOLDIER Yield, or thou diest.   **To Lucilius**
LUCILIUS Only I yield to die:
        There is so much that thou wilt kill me straight: **Offers money?**
15   Kill Brutus, and be honoured in his death.
FIRST SOLDIER We must not: a noble prisoner!
Enter Antony
SECOND SOLDIER Room, ho: tell Antony, Brutus is ta'en.

107 fellow equal   110 Thasos island in the north of the Aegean sea, not far from Philippi
112 discomfort dishearten   114 battles battalions   116 try test   5.4   2 bastard i.e. base person, one
who is no legitimate Roman   4 Marcus Cato also Portia's father   7 I am Brutus Lucilius lies in order to
confuse the enemy and protect Brutus   13 Only . . . die I yield only to die   14 so much either Lucilius offers
the soldier money or he refers to the abundance of honour to be gained from killing Brutus   straight
straight away   17 Room, ho make room

FIRST SOLDIER I'll tell the news. Here comes the general.
Brutus is ta'en, Brutus is ta'en, my lord.
20 **ANTONY** Where is he?
LUCILIUS Safe, Antony, Brutus is safe enough:
I dare assure thee that no enemy
Shall ever take alive the noble Brutus:
The gods defend him from so great a shame!
25 When you do find him, or alive or dead,
He will be found like Brutus, like himself.
ANTONY This is not Brutus, friend, but, I assure you,   *To First Soldier*
A prize no less in worth. Keep this man safe,
Give him all kindness. I had rather have
30 Such men my friends than enemies. Go on,
And see whe'er Brutus be alive or dead,
And bring us word unto Octavius' tent
How everything is chanced.   *Exeunt*

[Act 5 Scene 5]   *running scene 10 continues*

Enter Brutus, Dardanius, Clitus, Strato and Volumnius

BRUTUS Come, poor remains of friends, rest on this rock.   *Sits*
CLITUS Statilius showed the torch-light, but, my lord,
He came not back: he is or ta'en or slain.
BRUTUS Sit thee down, Clitus: slaying is the word.
5 It is a deed in fashion. Hark thee, Clitus.   *Whispers*
CLITUS What, I, my lord? No, not for all the world.
BRUTUS Peace then, no words.
CLITUS I'll rather kill myself.
BRUTUS Hark thee, Dardanius.   *Whispers*
10 **DARDANIUS** Shall I do such a deed?
CLITUS O Dardanius!
DARDANIUS O Clitus!
CLITUS What ill request did Brutus make to thee?
DARDANIUS To kill him, Clitus. Look, he meditates.
15 **CLITUS** Now is that noble vessel full of grief,
That it runs over even at his eyes.
BRUTUS Come hither, good Volumnius, list a word.
VOLUMNIUS What says my lord?
BRUTUS Why this, Volumnius:
20 The ghost of Caesar hath appeared to me

25 **or** either   33 **is chanced** has fallen out, come to pass   **5.5   1 remains** remnants, survivors
2 **showed the torch-light** i.e. signalled to show that he had completed his reconnaissance mission
17 **list** hear

Two several times by night: at Sardis once,
And this last night, here in Philippi fields:
I know my hour is come.

VOLUMNIUS Not so, my lord.

25   **BRUTUS** Nay, I am sure it is, Volumnius.
Thou seest the world, Volumnius, how it goes.
Our enemies have beat us to the pit: *Low alarums*
It is more worthy to leap in ourselves
Than tarry till they push us. Good Volumnius,

30   Thou know'st that we two went to school together:
Even for that our love of old, I prithee
Hold thou my sword-hilts, whilst I run on it.

VOLUMNIUS That's not an office for a friend, my lord.

Alarum still

CLITUS Fly, fly, my lord, there is no tarrying here.

35   **BRUTUS** Farewell to you, and you, and you,   *Addressing Clitus,*
Volumnius.—   *Dardanius, Volumnius*
Strato, thou hast been all this while asleep: *and Strato in turn*
Farewell to thee too, Strato.— Countrymen,
My heart doth joy that yet in all my life
I found no man but he was true to me.

40   I shall have glory by this losing day
More than Octavius and Mark Antony
By this vile conquest shall attain unto.
So fare you well at once, for Brutus' tongue
Hath almost ended his life's history:

45   Night hangs upon mine eyes, my bones would rest,
That have but laboured to attain this hour.

Alarum. Cry within: 'Fly fly fly!'

CLITUS Fly, my lord, fly!

BRUTUS Hence: I will follow.

            [*Exeunt Clitus, Dardanius and Volumnius*]
I prithee, Strato, stay thou by thy lord.

50   Thou art a fellow of a good respect:
Thy life hath had some smatch of honour in it.
Hold then my sword, and turn away thy face,
While I do run upon it. Wilt thou, Strato?

STRATO Give me your hand first. Fare you well, my lord.

---

21 **several** separate   27 **beat** driven   **pit** trap for animals/grave   29 **tarry** wait   31 **that**...**old** that old
friendship of ours   32 **sword-hilts** sword handle   33 **office** task   33 *still* continuing   42 **vile** ignoble,
morally reprehensible   46 **but**...**hour** toiled with the sole aim of finding death/done nothing other than toil
to arrive at this point   50 **respect** reputation   51 **smatch** smack, taste

55 **BRUTUS** Farewell, good Strato.—   *Runs on his sword*
                                     Caesar, now be still:
       I killed not thee with half so good a will.   *Dies*
       Alarum. Retreat. Enter Antony, Octavius, Messala, Lucilius
       and the army
       OCTAVIUS What man is that?
       MESSALA My master's man. Strato, where is thy master?
       STRATO Free from the bondage you are in, Messala,
60   The conquerors can but make a fire of him:
       For Brutus only overcame himself,
       And no man else hath honour by his death.
       LUCILIUS So Brutus should be found. I thank thee,
           Brutus,
       That thou hast proved Lucilius' saying true.
65 **OCTAVIUS** All that served Brutus, I will entertain them.
       Fellow, wilt thou bestow thy time with me?
       STRATO Ay, if Messala will prefer me to you.
       OCTAVIUS Do so, good Messala.
       MESSALA How died my master, Strato?
70 **STRATO** I held the sword and he did run on it.
       MESSALA Octavius, then take him to follow thee,
       That did the latest service to my master.
       ANTONY This was the noblest Roman of them all:
       All the conspirators save only he
75   Did that they did in envy of great Caesar.
       He only, in a general honest thought
       And common good to all, made one of them.
       His life was gentle, and the elements
       So mixed in him that Nature might stand up
80   And say to all the world 'This was a man!'
       OCTAVIUS According to his virtue let us use him
       With all respect and rites of burial.
       Within my tent his bones tonight shall lie,
       Most like a soldier, ordered honourably.
85   So call the field to rest, and let's away,
       To part the glories of this happy day.   *Exeunt*

---

55 **still** at peace 56 ***Retreat*** signal for the pursuing troops to cease 58 **man** servant 60 **make** . . . **him** i.e. cremate his body 61 **only** alone **overcame** conquered 63 **So** in just such a way 65 **entertain** employ 67 **prefer** recommend 72 **latest** last 75 **that** what **envy of** malice towards/jealousy of 76 **He** . . . **them** he alone joined the conspiracy out of honourable concern for the common good **honest** honourable/genuine 78 **gentle** noble **elements** i.e. of the universe (air, earth, fire and water)/of 'bodily humours' 79 **mixed** (harmoniously) combined 81 **use** treat 84 **ordered** treated 85 **field** battlefield 86 **part** share out

TEXTUAL NOTES

F = First Folio text of 1623
F2 = a correction introduced in the Second Folio text of 1632
F3 = a correction introduced in the Third Folio text of 1663–64
Ed = a correction introduced by a later editor
SH = speech heading (i.e. speaker's name)

List of parts = Ed

1.2.258 swoon *spelled* swound *in* F **310 digest** = Ed. F = disgest
1.3.21 glazed = F. *Sometimes emended to* glared **134 In favour's like** = Ed. F = Is Fauors, like
2.1.257 wafture = Ed. F = wafter **278 his** = Ed. F = hit **292 the** = Ed. F = tho **327 SH LIGARIUS** = Ed. F = *Cai. (throughout scene)*
2.2.48 are = Ed. F = heare
2.3.1 SH ARTEMIDORUS = Ed. *Not in* F
3.1.123 states = F2. F = State **125 lies** = F2. F = lye **273 SH ANTONY** = Ed. *Not in* F **294 SD *Octavius'*** = Ed. F = *Octavio's* **302 for** = F2. F = from
3.2.216 SH ALL = Ed. *Lines assigned to the* Second Plebeian *in* F **233 wit** = F2. F = writ
4.2.37 SH FIRST SOLDIER = Ed. *Not in* F **38 SH SECOND SOLDIER** = Ed. *Not in* F **39 SH THIRD SOLDIER** = Ed. *Not in* F **105 budge** *spelled* bouge *in* F **248 tenor** *spelled* Tenure *in* F **339 will** = F2. F = will it **385 Lucius** *spelled Lucus in* F
5.1.44 teeth = F3. F = teethes **91 steads** *spelled* steeds *in* F
5.3.103 whe'er = Ed. F = where **105 fare** = Ed. F = far **107 more** = Ed. F = mo **110 Thasos** = Ed *(after Plutarch).* F = *Tharsus* **114 Flavius** = F2. F = *Flavio*
5.4.7 SH LUCILIUS = Ed. *Not in* F **12 SH FIRST SOLDIER** = Ed. F = *Sold.* **18 tell the** = Ed. F = tell thee **31 whe'er** = Ed. F = where

SCENE-BY-SCENE
ANALYSIS

ACT 1 SCENE 1

Flavius and Murellus tell the commoners they should be working and that they should carry the 'sign' of their 'profession' with them at all times. The cobbler explains that they are going to see Caesar make his triumphant return after defeating Pompey. Murellus is scornful, pointing out that Caesar brings back no 'conquest' or 'tributaries'. He reminds the commoners of their previous allegiance to Pompey, drawing attention to the shifting loyalties/betrayal of the times. Murellus' speech also introduces the significance of rhetoric and the power of language, particularly in public address. Flavius commands the commoners to 'weep' into the Tiber for Pompey, accusing them of being 'tongue-tied in their guiltiness', again drawing our attention to the importance of language/speech, but also to guilt/complicity. Flavius suggests that he and Murellus remove the adornments from the statues of Caesar, warning that Caesar 'would soar above the view of men' to keep the people of Rome 'in servile fearfulness'.

ACT 1 SCENE 2

Lines 1–28: Caesar and others prepare to watch a course run as part of the feast of Lupercal. Antony is to run the course, and Caesar tells Calpurnia to stand where Antony can reach her, as it is believed the touch of a runner in the 'holy chase' can cure sterility. He reminds Antony of this, and Antony replies, 'When Caesar says, "Do this" it is performed', demonstrating Antony's loyalty and Caesar's authority. A soothsayer calls out to Caesar, 'Beware the Ides of

March', and repeats his warning, but Caesar dismisses it, perhaps revealing his arrogance. In any case, it is the first of many complicated incidents in the play which seem concerned with the tensions between fate and free will and the significance of omens and prophecies.

Lines 29–183: As the others leave to watch the course, Cassius and Brutus remain. Cassius suggests that Brutus has grown distant, reminding him of their past friendship. Brutus assures him that if he has recently 'veiled' his looks, it is only because he is 'with himself at war', and 'Vexed' inside, introducing the conflict of public and private. Cassius tells Brutus that the most respected citizens of Rome, 'groaning underneath this age's yoke', admire him and look to him. Brutus is wary, saying that Cassius is asking him to recognize a quality within himself that he does not possess, but Cassius continues to flatter, offering to be Brutus' 'glass', so that he can 'discover' these qualities within himself. As they talk, a fanfare and shouting are heard and Brutus says he fears the people have made Caesar king. Cassius seizes on this and asks whether or not this is what Brutus would want, forcing him to acknowledge that, despite his love for Caesar, he does not want him as king. He questions whether what Cassius has to say relates to 'the general good', revealing genuine concern for the welfare of Rome. He assures Cassius that he loves 'honour' more than he fears death. Cassius says that this shows Brutus' 'virtue' and argues that they were both 'born free as Caesar' and that he cannot bring himself to be 'In awe of such a thing as I myself', complaining that Caesar has 'now become a god', despite his many weaknesses.

They hear another shout, and Brutus suggests that 'new honours' are being 'heaped on Caesar'. Cassius argues that Caesar is now a 'Colossus', while they are merely 'petty men'. He adds that 'Men at some time are masters of their fates', drawing attention again to the conflict between free will and fate. He returns to the subject of Rome, playing on Brutus' concerns for the civic good rather than personal triumph. He reminds him of another Brutus, who overthrew the last king of Rome and established the republic. Brutus assures Cassius that he has already thought 'of this and of these times'. He will not discuss it further now, but promises that they will talk again.

Lines 184–220: Caesar and his train return. Cassius quickly advises Brutus to 'pluck Casca by the sleeve' to find out what has happened. Brutus observes that Caesar looks angry and that Calpurnia is pale. Caesar asks Antony to ensure that he only has 'fat / Sleek-headed men' about him, unlike Cassius, who has 'a lean and hungry look' and is 'dangerous'. Antony reassures Caesar that Cassius is 'a noble Roman', but Caesar says that he mistrusts him. Unlike Antony, he does not care for plays or music and seldom smiles. Caesar observes that men such as Cassius are 'never at heart's ease / Whiles they behold a greater than themselves'. He asks Antony for his opinion, requesting him to speak on his right side as he is deaf in his left ear, another subtle reference to Caesar's weaknesses, and a metaphorical allusion to his lack of perception/understanding. He exits with his train, leaving Brutus, Cassius and Casca.

Lines 221–331: Casca describes how Caesar was offered a crown three times by Antony, and that each time he refused it to cheers from the crowd. He adds, however, that he thinks Caesar 'would fain have had it' and 'was very loath to lay his fingers off it'. As the crowd 'hooted' and 'clapped', Caesar swooned and fell down, 'foamed at mouth, and was speechless'. Brutus explains that Caesar 'hath the falling sickness' (epilepsy), again drawing attention to potential infirmities. Casca goes on to describe how Caesar was so much in favour with the crowd that they were not put off by his collapse, although it appears to have affected his mood. Before leaving, Casca adds that Murellus and Flavius have been 'put to silence' for 'pulling scarves off Caesar's images'. Brutus comments on how 'blunt' Casca is, but Cassius says this is 'put on'. Brutus promises to speak to Cassius the next day, and leaves. Alone, Cassius muses on Brutus' 'noble' nature, but feels that he can be manipulated. He reveals his plan to throw forged letters through Brutus' window, complaining of 'Caesar's ambition'.

ACT 1 SCENE 3

Lines 1–41: Casca and Cicero meet during a violent storm. Cicero is unmoved, but Casca is disturbed by the 'tempest', which he sees as portentous. Questioned by Cicero, he lists recent omens, such as a man whose hand burned 'Like twenty torches', but who remained 'unscorched'. Cicero agrees but points out that people misinterpret things. Casca tells Cicero that Caesar will be at the Capitol the next day, and Cicero bids him goodnight.

Lines 42–170: Cassius arrives, and Casca comments again on the 'menace' of the heavens. Like Cicero, Cassius is unconcerned, describing how he presented himself to 'the aim and very flash' of the lightning. Casca warns that he should not 'tempt the heavens': men should 'fear and tremble' when the 'most mighty gods' send such 'tokens'. Cassius argues that Casca should ask himself why the heavens have sent 'instruments of fear and warning'. Casca understands that Cassius refers to Caesar, and reports that the senators mean to make him king the next day. Cassius declares that he will 'deliver' himself from such bondage, and calls upon the gods. Casca argues that he, too, can 'cancel his captivity'. Cassius tells Casca that he has the support of several 'noblest-minded Romans' to undertake 'an enterprise / Of honourable dangerous consequence', and that they are waiting for him under the cover of the 'fearful night'. They are interrupted by the arrival of Cinna, and draw back until Cassius identifies him. Cassius asks whether the conspirators are waiting, then sends Cinna with the letters to throw into Brutus' house. He asks Casca to accompany him to see Brutus. Casca observes that Brutus' involvement will make their 'offence' appear as 'virtue' and 'worthiness', because the people love and respect him.

ACT 2 SCENE 1

Lines 1–59: Brutus is in his orchard, unable to sleep. He sends Lucius to light a candle in his study. Brutus' soliloquy reveals his concerns over Caesar: he can see no other way to stop him than 'by his death'. He makes it clear that his reasons are not 'personal', but 'general'. He concedes that he has never known Caesar to allow his 'affections' to be 'swayed / More than his reason', but adds that ambition is dangerous. Lucius returns with a letter he has found in the study (one of those planted by Cassius and Cinna), and Brutus sends him away again to check tomorrow's date. Alone, he reads the letter. The audience only receives brief words and phrases: 'Shall Rome, etc.', 'Speak, strike, redress', contributing to a sense of Brutus' fragmented thoughts, but suggesting doubt as to how convincing the letter is, and the extent to which Brutus is willing to 'piece it out' to persuade himself. He is resolved, however: he promises Rome that 'redress will follow'. Lucius returns with the information that the next day is 15 March and goes to answer a knocking at the gate.

Lines 60–243: Lucius announces that Cassius has arrived with others whose 'hats are plucked about their ears / And half their faces buried in their cloaks'. Unsettled, Brutus tells Lucius to show them in. Cassius introduces the other conspirators, assuring Brutus that they all 'honour' him, as does 'every noble Roman'. Cassius and Brutus speak aside before Brutus asks everyone to give him their hands. Cassius wishes to 'swear [their] resolution', but Brutus insists there will be no 'oath': none is needed if they are all acting as 'countrymen' and 'Romans'. Cassius argues that Antony should also be killed, but Brutus points out that this will make them seem 'too bloody': they must be 'sacrificers, but not butchers', and their 'purpose necessary, and not envious'. The clock strikes three, and the conspirators arrange that they will all meet to accompany Caesar to the Capitol by 'the eighth hour'. Metellus suggests that they include Ligarius, and Brutus asks him to send Ligarius to him. He encourages the others to conceal their true feelings as 'actors do', and they leave. Lucius does not answer Brutus' call, and Brutus envies him his peaceful sleep.

Lines 244–350: Portia enters, worried about her husband, and the dynamics of the scene shift from political to domestic/personal. Brutus is concerned that Portia's health will suffer in the 'raw cold morning'. She comments on his recent behaviour, observing that whatever is troubling him prevents him from eating, talking or sleeping. She begs him to tell her his 'cause of grief'. Kneeling, she argues that he cannot be ill, but that he must have 'some sick offence within [his] mind', and asks him to tell her. Their exchange is tender, in contrast to the earlier brutal plotting. Brutus assures her that she is his 'true and honourable wife' and that he will explain 'the secrets of [his] heart' in a little while. As she leaves, Lucius shows in Ligarius, who assures Brutus that he will 'discard' his sickness to follow him.

ACT 2 SCENE 2

Lines 1–59: Like Brutus, Caesar has had a troubled night. Calpurnia has dreamed three times of Caesar's murder, calling out in her sleep. As Caesar sends a servant to the priests, instructing them to make a sacrifice to determine his success that day, Calpurnia enters. Their conversation highlights tensions between public and domestic/ personal concerns, as Calpurnia begs Caesar to remain at home. She tells him of the various omens that have been seen, but Caesar argues that what is 'purposed by the mighty gods' cannot be avoided, and that the 'predictions' do not necessarily relate to him. Like Portia, Calpurnia kneels before her husband, asking him to send Antony to the senate to say he is unwell. He agrees.

Lines 60–136: Decius arrives to fetch Caesar, but Caesar asks him to tell the senate he 'will not come'. When Decius asks for a reason, Caesar declares that it should be enough for the senate that it is his 'will' not to. He explains to Decius, however, about Calpurnia's dream: she saw a statue of Caesar 'Which, like a fountain with an hundred spouts, / Did run pure blood' that Roman citizens bathed their hands in. Decius suggests that they have misinterpreted the dream: it means that 'great Rome shall suck / Reviving blood' from Caesar. Caesar is impressed by his reasoning, and Decius tells him that the senate has decided to give 'a crown to mighty Caesar' today, arguing that they may change their minds if he does not go and that he will look foolish. Caesar is ashamed of yielding to Calpurnia, and decides to go. Brutus and others join the scene, coming also to fetch Caesar, who ironically refers to them as his 'friends'.

ACT 2 SCENE 3

Artemidorus reads the petition he plans to hand to Caesar, warning him against the conspirators.

ACT 2 SCENE 4

Portia struggles between her fears for Brutus and her promise to 'keep counsel'. The Soothsayer enters on his way to deliver a suit to Caesar advising him 'to befriend himself' and Portia betrays her nerves as she questions him.

ACT 3 SCENE 1

Lines 1–84: As Caesar approaches the Capitol, he observes that the 'Ides of March have come' but the Soothsayer points out that they are not yet over. Artemidorus attempts to present his petition to Caesar, but he refuses to listen. The senators hustle Artemidorus away. The tension is marked as the senators worry that they have been found out. However, Trebonius draws Antony 'out of the way', and Caesar settles to hear the business of the senate. Metellus kneels and begins to flatter Caesar, asking that his brother's banishment be repealed, but Caesar interrupts, saying that he will not hear 'base spaniel-fawning', and refuses to reconsider. One by one the senators kneel before Caesar in an ironic reversal of the true power dynamics at play, and add their word to that of Metellus. Caesar, however, says that he is as 'constant as the northern star' and refuses to change his mind. When Cinna also kneels, Caesar asks if they will 'lift up Olympus', emphasizing his sense of self-importance. Casca stabs Caesar while the other conspirators rush in, following in a frenzied attack (Octavius later speaks of 'Caesar's three and thirty wounds': 5.1.55). Brutus is the last to strike, and Caesar's final words, '*Et tu, Brute?*', reveal his shock at his friend's betrayal.

Lines 85–159: Cinna cries out 'Tyranny is dead!' and calls for it to be proclaimed in the streets. Everyone except the conspirators and Publius leaves during the chaos, including Antony, who Trebonius reports has 'Fled to his house amazed'. Publius is urged to go as Brutus argues that none but those who have committed the deed shall be punished for it. He tells his fellow-conspirators to 'stoop' and 'bathe' their hands in Caesar's blood, echoing Calpurnia's dream. They plan to walk to the market-place, showing their bloody hands and swords and declaring 'Peace, freedom and liberty!' In a moment of meta-theatre, they imagine their 'lofty scene' being acted out in years to come, with themselves portrayed as 'The men that gave their country liberty'. A servant brings a message from Antony. Casting himself at their feet, he says that Antony 'bid' him to say that 'Brutus is noble, wise, valiant and honest' and that he asks to be allowed to approach in safety and be given reasons for Caesar's murder. Despite Cassius' misgivings, Brutus agrees and gives his word that Antony shall not be harmed.

Lines 160–272: Antony arrives and addresses his first words to 'mighty' Caesar's body, before saying that if they intend to kill him too, they should do so now with their swords, 'made rich / With the most noble blood of all this world'. Brutus assures him that although their hands seem 'bloody and cruel', their hearts are 'pitiful'. He asks Antony to wait until they have reassured the frightened crowd and promises to explain why he killed Caesar even though he loved him. Antony shakes hands with each conspirator in turn then addresses Caesar's corpse again, ensuring that the audience's attention and sympathy is with Caesar as he describes himself as 'Shaking the bloody fingers' of Caesar's 'foes', comparing them to hunters and Caesar to a slaughtered deer. Cassius insists that they do not blame Antony for praising Caesar, but that they want to know whether they can count him as a friend. He reassures them but asks again for their 'reasons', and that he may be allowed to carry Caesar's body to the market-place and to speak at his funeral. Brutus agrees but Cassius is concerned. Cassius advises Brutus not to allow Antony to speak as the people will be 'moved' by him. Brutus decides that he will address the crowd first, telling them that Antony is speaking with his permission. Antony agrees to this and they leave him with Caesar's body.

Lines 273–316: Antony apologizes to Caesar for being 'meek and gentle with these butchers', revealing his true pain and anger. He makes a prophecy that there will be 'fierce civil strife' throughout Italy. He paints a bloody and violent picture, claiming that 'Caesar's spirit' will roam looking for 'revenge'. A Servant arrives from Octavius Caesar, bringing news of his imminent arrival. The Servant sees Caesar's body and begins to weep, causing Antony to shed tears as well. Antony tells the Servant to warn Octavius that Rome is dangerous, but first to help carry Caesar's body to the pulpit and stay to hear Antony's funeral speech.

ACT 3 SCENE 2

Lines 1–68: In the Forum, the plebeians demand an explanation. Brutus announces that he will speak to some of the crowd, while Cassius addresses others elsewhere. Brutus' speech combines rhetorical devices with prose to appeal to his plebeian audience. He argues that he loved Rome more than Caesar, and asks them whether they would rather Caesar was living and that they were 'slaves', or that they were free and Casear dead. The crowd are swayed and, as Antony enters with Caesar's body, call out for Brutus to be 'crowned'. Brutus silences them, and, before he leaves, asks that they stay to hear Antony, who has the senate's 'permission' to address them.

Lines 69–180: The crowd is hostile, but Antony's speech is powerful and emotive, and his rhetoric more sophisticated. He praises Brutus, reiterating that he is 'an honourable man', although his repetition seems to undermine rather than reinforce the statement. He reminds them of Caesar's qualities and his previous refusal of the 'kingly crown'. He breaks off, apparently overcome with emotion, and the crowd show how his words have moved them, declaring that Caesar was wronged, and that there is 'not a nobler man in Rome than Antony'. Antony reveals that he has Caesar's will, although he 'must not' read it. The crowd want to hear it, but Antony claims that it will 'wrong the honourable men / Whose daggers have stabbed Caesar'; his use of 'honourable' becoming more sardonic with every repetition. The crowd have been won over: Brutus and the others are 'traitors', 'villains' and 'murderers'. They demand to hear the will, and Antony, with careful humility, asks their permission to come down among them, and that they form a ring around Caesar's body.

Lines 181–285: Showing his absolute control over the mood of the crowd, Antony tells them to 'prepare to shed' tears, reminiscing about the first time that Caesar wore the cloak that covers him. He points out each stab wound, listing the men who gave them and calling Brutus' 'the most unkindest cut of all'. Finally, he reveals Caesar's body to the crowd. They weep for Caesar, and call for revenge but Antony claims that he does not wish to create a mutiny. His careful denials inflame the crowd further, and to reinforce this, he reads them the will in which Caesar has left each Roman citizen seventy-five drachmas as well as all his 'private arbours and new-planted orchards' in which they may 'walk abroad and recreate' themselves. Roused, the plebeians plan to burn Caesar's body 'in the holy place', before burning the conspirators' houses. They take Caesar's body and Antony remains, calling for the ensuing chaos to 'Take . . . what course thou wilt'. Octavius' servant returns with the news that he is already in Rome, with Lepidus at Caesar's house.

ACT 3 SCENE 3

The plebeians kill Cinna the Poet, even though he explains that he is not 'Cinna the conspirator', demonstrating the anarchic brutality that now prevails.

ACT 4 SCENE 1

Antony, Octavius and Lepidus discuss which conspirators are to die, including Lepidus' brother and Antony's nephew. Antony asks Lepidus to go to Caesar's house to collect the will. Once Lepidus has gone, he calls him 'a slight unmeritable man', and questions his abilities as one of a triumvirate. He suggests that Lepidus' role is merely to take on the burden of the tasks that they don't want to do themselves, like an 'ass' to be 'led or driven' as Octavius and Antony see fit. Despite Octavius' comments that Lepidus is 'a tried and valiant soldier', Antony continues to belittle him, foreshadowing the future in which Rome will have another divided, and therefore potentially weak, leadership. Their talk turns to Brutus and Cassius, who are making preparations to fight. They resolve to go and do likewise.

ACT 4 SCENE 2

Lines 1–214: Brutus awaits Cassius. Lucilius arrives and tells him that Cassius, while courteous and respectful, was not as open and friendly towards him as he once was. Brutus agrees, saying that Cassius is 'cooling' in his friendship and hides behind 'enforced ceremony'. Cassius arrives and directly accuses Brutus of wronging him and hiding his true feelings behind his 'sober form'. Brutus says that they should not be seen arguing and invites Cassius to his tent. Once inside, Cassius accuses Brutus of disgracing Lucius Pella for accepting bribes from the Sardians, despite the fact that Cassius himself defended Pella. Brutus argues that Cassius dishonoured himself in defending him. Brutus reminds Cassius that they killed Caesar because he was likely to become corrupt, and claims that they must not then be corrupt themselves. The argument escalates and the political accusations become mixed with personal insults until Cassius offers Brutus his dagger, telling him to 'Strike as thou didst at Caesar'. Brutus says that Cassius is too hot-tempered and they are reconciled, embracing each other, and Cassius asks Brutus to bear with his 'rash humour'. They are interrupted by a Poet demanding to see them. The Poet warns them that they should 'Love and be friends', but he is dismissed. Lucilius and Titinius are sent with messages to the commanders.

Lines 215–326: Cassius expresses surprise at the depth of Brutus' anger, and Brutus reveals that Portia is dead. She has killed herself due to Brutus' absence, and fear of the growing strength of Antony and Octavius. His fragmented phrases reveal genuine sorrow, but he resolves that they will 'Speak no more of her' as Lucius brings wine and tapers. Brutus and Cassius drink to each other and are joined by Titinius and Messala. Brutus shows letters from which he has learned that the armies of Octavius and Antony are on their way to Philippi. Messala has had similar news and they both reveal that the triumvirs have executed up to a hundred senators, including Cicero. Tentatively, Messala asks Brutus if he has heard from Portia, before revealing what Brutus already knows of her death. Again, Brutus does not dwell on this, saying that he has 'the patience to endure it now' before changing the subject to the battle they must fight. He asks whether they should march to Philippi. Cassius suggests that they let the enemy come to them, so that their troops will be weary while their own will be 'full of rest, defence and nimbleness'. Once again, Brutus and Cassius are in disagreement, but Cassius bows to Brutus' suggestion and agrees to go to Philippi. The leaders bid each other goodnight.

Lines 327–401: Brutus instructs Varrus and Claudio to sleep in his tent in case he has messages for Cassius. His exchange with Lucius reveals a gentler, more compassionate side. Lucius falls asleep. The Ghost of Caesar appears, announcing that it is Brutus' 'evil spirit' and telling him that it shall appear again 'at Philippi'. It vanishes before Brutus can talk with it further, and he calls out to wake Lucius, Varrus and Claudio. They all deny either crying out or seeing anything, and Brutus sends Lucius and Varrus to Cassius, telling him to be ready to march early in the morning.

ACT 5 SCENE 1

At Philippi, Octavius and Antony discuss the approach of the enemy. Echoing the divisions in the conspirators' camp, they briefly disagree over tactics before marching. Brutus and Cassius enter with their armies, and the two sets of leaders meet in 'parley', exchanging insults that focus attention on the theme of speech or 'words'.

Octavius and Antony lead their armies away. Brutus calls Lucilius, and the two speak apart as Cassius reveals his own concerns to Messala: despite not previously believing in such things, he is unnerved by several omens they encountered on their march to Philippi. Brutus returns, and he and Cassius contemplate what will happen if they lose. Brutus vows that he will not be taken captive to Rome. They say farewell, and go into battle.

ACT 5 SCENE 2

Brutus sends Messala with messages to Cassius: he can see a possible weakness in Octavius' army and is going to attack.

ACT 5 SCENE 3

Lines 1–51: Cassius watches as his own troops run. Titinius blames Brutus for attacking Octavius too soon while Cassius' troops were surrounded by Antony's. Pindarus arrives, urging Cassius to flee, as Antony has entered the camp. Cassius assures him that he is far enough away and sends Titinius for news. He sends Pindarus further up the hill to observe the battlefield, before noting that it is his birthday and likely also to be the day he dies: 'where I did begin, there shall I end'. Pindarus reports what he believes he can see: Titinius surrounded by horsemen, who kill him. Ashamed of what he perceives as his own cowardice, Cassius calls Pindarus to him and reminds him of the oath he made to do whatever Cassius bid him to. Cassius hands Pindarus his sword and tells him to kill him, thus rendering Pindarus a 'freeman' and giving Caesar his revenge. Pindarus does so and flees.

Lines 52–116: Titinius and Messala are discussing the battle, hoping that their tidings will 'comfort Cassius'. They see his body and, lamenting, Messala goes to tell Brutus. Titinius addresses Cassius' body, laying on it a wreath of victory that Brutus had sent for him. He guesses that Cassius has 'misconstrued everything' he has seen and heard of the battle, echoing earlier references to the potential to misinterpret events. Titinius stabs himself. Brutus is led in by Messala and, seeing the bodies, claims that the spirit of Caesar 'walks abroad'. Promising Cassius that he will 'find time' to mourn him, Brutus orders the bodies to be sent to Thasos.

ACT 5 SCENE 4

Brutus rallies his men and exits, fighting. Young Cato fights bravely before he is killed. Lucilius pretends to be Brutus and is taken prisoner. Antony arrives, and his soldiers tell him that they have Brutus. Lucilius claims that Brutus is now 'safe enough'. Antony praises Lucilius' bravery, ordering his men to treat him well.

ACT 5 SCENE 5

Brutus asks his followers to kill him but they refuse. He tells Volumnius of the visions he has had of Caesar's ghost, saying that he knows his 'hour is come'. Increasing alarums are heard and Brutus' followers urge him to flee, but he bids them farewell in turn. Strato remains and holds Brutus' sword for him to run onto. He dies as Antony and Octavius arrive and Strato claims that Brutus is now 'free', having given no man the 'honour' of his death but himself. Antony says of Brutus that he was 'the noblest Roman of them all' and that he alone among the conspirators killed Caesar in the belief that it was for the 'common good', and was not driven by envy. Octavius agrees, and declares that Brutus will be given burial honours befitting a soldier.

JULIUS CAESAR
IN PERFORMANCE:
THE RSC AND BEYOND

The best way to understand a Shakespeare play is to see it or ideally to participate in it. By examining a range of productions, we may gain a sense of the extraordinary variety of approaches and interpretations that are possible – a variety that gives Shakespeare his unique capacity to be reinvented and made 'our contemporary' four centuries after his death.

We begin with a brief overview of the play's theatrical and cinematic life, offering historical perspectives on how it has been performed. We then analyse in more detail a series of productions staged over the last half-century by the Royal Shakespeare Company. The sense of dialogue between productions that can only occur when a company is dedicated to the revival and investigation of the Shakespeare canon over a long period, together with the uniquely comprehensive archival resource of promptbooks, programme notes, reviews and interviews held on behalf of the RSC at the Shakespeare Birthplace Trust in Stratford-upon-Avon, allows an 'RSC stage history' to become a crucible in which the chemistry of the play can be explored.

Finally, we go to the horse's mouth. Modern theatre is dominated by the figure of the director, who must hold together the whole play, whereas the actor must concentrate on his or her part. The director's viewpoint is therefore especially valuable. Shakespeare's plasticity is wonderfully revealed when we hear directors of highly successful productions answering the same questions in very different ways.

FOUR CENTURIES OF *JULIUS CAESAR*: AN OVERVIEW

When Polonius tells Hamlet 'I did enact Julius Caesar. I was killed i'th'Capitol. Brutus killed me' (Act 3 scene 2), we hear what may be one of the earliest theatrical in-jokes. The actor playing Polonius (probably John Hemings) is almost certainly referring to the Lord Chamberlain's Men's recent *Julius Caesar* and his own role as Caesar. In reminding Hamlet of his assassination, we are reminded that Richard Burbage, playing Hamlet, had almost certainly played Brutus. In *Hamlet*, then, 'Brutus' re-enacts his murder of 'Caesar', only behind an arras instead of in the Capitol. The expectation that audiences would be familiar with the recent play is an early indication of the extraordinary popularity of *Julius Caesar*, a popularity that rarely diminished over the centuries.

Julius Caesar was first performed at the Globe, and may even have opened the company's new home. The Swiss scholar and writer Thomas Platter provides a rare eye-witness account of a Globe performance, though it is the closing jig that commands his attention:

> In the strewn roof-house [I] saw the tragedy of the first Emperor Julius with at least fifteen characters very well acted. At the end of the comedy they danced according to their custom with extreme elegance.[1]

Evidence of court performances in 1613, 1637 and 1638 suggests ongoing popularity through the reigns of James I and Charles I. It was the relationship between Brutus and Cassius, particularly the 'quarrel scene' of Act 4 scene 3, that appears to have captured the public's imagination:

> So have I seen, when Caesar would appear,
> And on the Stage at half-sword parley were
> *Brutus* and *Cassius*: oh how the Audience,
> Were ravish'd, with what wonder they went thence.[2]

The play's later production history is characterized by strikingly varied political appropriations, both inciting and warning against revolution. This inherent adaptability allowed *Caesar* to flourish in an unusually intact form: the text published 'As it is now ACTED/AT THE/ Theatre Royal'[3] around 1684 closely followed the Folio with the exception of some reassigning of speeches. Most notably, Casca replaced Murellus in the opening scene, strengthening the prominence of this perennially popular character.

The play was assigned to Thomas Killigrew's King's Company following the reopening of the theatres after the Restoration of Charles II in 1660. The earliest cast list shows Charles Hart as Brutus, Michael Mohun as Cassius and Edward Kynaston, formerly celebrated for his female roles, as Antony. This was probably the cast that performed before royalty in 1676. By the 1680s, Thomas Betterton was playing Brutus at Drury Lane, a role he continued in until 1707. Betterton's role-making performance was described as of 'unruffled Temper... his steady Look alone supply'd that Terror which he disdain'd an Intemperance in his Voice should rise to'.[4]

By 1707, the play was at the Queen's Theatre, subtitled 'With The Death of Brutus And Cassius'. Betterton was succeeded by Barton Booth, playing opposite Robert Wilks' Antony. The popularity of *Caesar*, however, transcended individual playhouses or actors. Politically, its 'message' of liberty and personal justice cast Brutus as patriot, as acknowledged by a 1707 prologue spoken by 'The Ghost of Shakespear':

> Then I brought mighty Julius on the stage,
> Then Britain heard my godlike Roman's rage,
> And came in crowds, with rapture came, to see,
> The world from its proud tyrant freed by me.
> Rome he enslav'd, for which he died once there;
> But for his introducing slav'ry here,
> Ten times I sacrifice him ev'ry year.[5]

Caesar was understood as a tyrannous villain while Brutus was a hero of righteous action, and it was his conflicts – both internal and with Cassius – that increasingly generated interest. In 1710, the 'quarrel scene' was even performed as a stand-alone piece at Greenwich.[6]

The adaptation by John Dryden and William Davenant published in 1719 touched the play 'comparatively lightly', cutting those sections 'which would tend to lower the heroic tone of the leading characters'[7], and Brutus in particular benefited from added lines that cast his dying moments as a patriotic suicide: 'Thus *Brutus* always strikes for Liberty.'[8]

Covent Garden dominated the play during the 1740s and 1750s, with Lacey Ryan a consistent Cassius playing alongside James Quin and Thomas Sheridan, among others, as Brutus. These illustrious names, however, couldn't prevent a sudden decline in the play's fortunes. The play limped on in increasingly infrequent performances until 1780. In 1770, meanwhile, the play crossed the Atlantic to Philadelphia, where an advertisement promised 'the noble struggles for liberty by that renowned patriot, Marcus Brutus'.[9] Brutus, understandably, became a revolutionary hero in young America.

Following a thirty-year absence from the London stage, John Philip Kemble's lavish 1812 production at Covent Garden remade the play as a spectacular with grand processions and displays. *Caesar* lent itself to the age's penchant for historical recreation, and Kemble's production renewed interest in the play for the nineteenth-century pictorial stage. In 1823, Henry Kemble played Brutus in *The Death of Caesar; or, the Battle of Philippi*, which retained the main events of the play but relatively little of Shakespeare's text. The next significant productions were those of William Charles Macready at Covent Garden (1838–39) and Drury Lane (1843), which utilized over a hundred extras 'to lend complementary interest to the major movement of any given scene'.[10] Macready believed the assassination of Caesar should be the true focal point of the play and used his enormous cast to make the murder truly public, beginning a process that subsequently allowed Antony to whip them into a terrifying simulation of mass rioting.

Samuel Phelps was Macready's Cassius, contrasting fieriness with Brutus' stoic calm, the classic dynamic of the pair. Phelps later directed several revivals in a similar vein at Sadler's Wells between 1846 and 1862. In 1868, meanwhile, *Caesar* was one of the earliest

Shakespeare plays adapted for the Japanese stage in a Kabuki-style production 'which served as a protest play against the bureaucratic "law and order" government'.[11] The international recognizability of its story and the potential for political appropriation allowed the play to cross cultural and linguistic borders.

Classic tragedy was dominated in late nineteenth-century America by the partnership of Lawrence Barrett and Edwin Booth. Booth's *Caesar* of 1871–72 in New York was his climactic achievement, both in its strong ensemble cast and its spectacular scenic set-pieces, including a ritual cremation for Brutus. 'Booth presented Brutus as the philosophical man rather than the warrior',[12] following historical record rather than the American stage convention of a passionate figure, for which he received criticism. Barrett, by contrast, was the age's defining Cassius: in the 1875 revival

> he presented Cassius with such subtlety of thought, such power of intellectual passion, such vigorous and sonorous eloquence, and such force of identification and spontaneity as could not, and did not, fail to command the warmest admiration and sympathy.[13]

In 1889 Osmond Tearle played Brutus in Stratford-upon-Avon, reviews of his performance articulating what was by now expected of the character. His performance was described as

> almost pre-Raphaelite in its attention to even the smallest detail . . . [he] brought out with rare skill the various phases of the character, the attributes of authority, suspicion, craft, super-stitious fear, being blent with dignity, a beautiful speciousness, consummate worldly tact, pusillanimity, and that histrionic faculty of being 'all things to all men'.[14]

The same critic accounted for weak performances in the female roles by suggesting that 'in Julius Caesar there is no great part in which an actress can particularly distinguish herself'.[15] Only in the later twentieth century would the roles of Portia and Calpurnia become more celebrated.

Herbert Beerbohm Tree's 1898 production at Her Majesty's was a triumph. The souvenir programme explained:

> At Her Majesty's it is not the historic band of conspirators that strikes the key note of the play. It is not even the mighty figure of Caesar treacherously brought low. It is the feverish, pulsing life of the imperial city.[16]

Beerbohm Tree's hundred-strong crowd dominated the Forum scene and Beerbohm Tree himself played Antony, orchestrating the crowd in a remarkable display of rhetoric and choreography. His choice to centralize Antony necessitated Charles Fulton's 'sympathetic and reformist Caesar',[17] so that Antony's loyalty could be laudable. The dynamic between Antony and the crowd has often since been choreographed to great effect, notably in Peter Stein's epic 1992 Salzburg production.

Frank Benson directed several productions at Stratford between 1892 and 1915, also playing Antony: 'his action was dignified, his delivery was marked by intensity, intellectual keenness, and impressiveness, and altogether it was a fine study and a striking example of effective and impassioned oratory'.[18] Otho Stuart was his best-received Brutus, his 'dignified self-possession and measured diction'[19] pairing especially well with Henry Ainley's vehement Cassius.

Beerbohm Tree and Benson's productions were pro-establishment in their sympathetic treatment of Caesar, and this conservative reading was effectively given royal approval on 2 May 1916. Shakespeare's tercentenary was celebrated with a Royal Matinee at Drury Lane, during which Benson – playing Caesar 'with consummate dignity'[20] – was called to the Royal Box and knighted.

William Bridges-Adams succeeded Benson at Stratford in 1919 and was the first director to restore a completely uncut text. Reviewers appreciated the additions: where Act 3 scene 1 had traditionally ended with 'Cry havoc and let slip the dogs of war', the restored scene with Octavius' servant 'gives the key to the future action of Mark Antony',[21] and allowed Bridges-Adams to begin questioning Caesar's motivations. Later developments included

1. Herbert Beerbohm Tree's production, 1898, Her Majesty's Theatre, with Lewis Miller as Brutus and Evelyn Millard as Portia.

Stanley Lothbury's 'querulous, snarling, decrepit old man' of a Caesar and Baliol Holloway's Antony as 'fawning demagogue' in 1922.[22] By 1934, John Wyse's Brutus 'seemed never more noble', while Eric Maxon's Caesar succeeded through 'restrained force of expression in making Caesar bigger than the Caesar Shakespeare drew'.[23] Iris Guillaume's Calpurnia was cast as a Mary Magdalene figure, though reviews still complained that 'women have little place in *Julius Caesar*'.[24] An 'interpolated picture of Antony viewing a burning Rome while a beggar clutches at his legs'[25] was, however, ridiculed.

The most influential stage production of the century, Orson Welles' *Julius Caesar: The Death of a Dictator*, opened at New York's Mercury Theater in November 1937. Welles 'set about to arouse the passions of his audience with a simulation of the chaos then overtaking Europe',[26] rendering the play terrifyingly relevant. The script was severely pared down to focus on Caesar, Brutus and the mob. One notable inclusion was the restoration of the lynching of Cinna the Poet: 'The Mercury audience made Cinna's experience their own, representing as it did their worst fears for themselves and for those dearest to them abroad.'[27] Welles' self-consciously theatrical production was performed in modern dress, deliberately evoking Mussolini and fascism to generate a sense of pity and horror at atrocities across the Atlantic. The production's backstage story was turned into a 2009 Hollywood movie, *Me and Orson Welles*. Anti-dictatorial readings of the play have since been commonplace: a 1969 production in Minneapolis was set in Latin America with Caesar as 'an aspiring sun-god in white and gold',[28] while in Miami in 1986 audiences were 'brought to their feet by the spectacle of the assassins bathing their hands in the blood of Caesar as Fidel Castro'.[29]

Also influential was Joseph L. Mankiewicz's 1953 motion picture starring James Mason (Brutus), John Gielgud (Cassius) and Marlon Brando (Antony). The Forum scene incorporated 1,200 extras, though the individual performances were praised as much as the grand spectacle. Gielgud played Cassius as 'the vulgar abstraction of personal jealousy',[30] while Brando's physical Antony was 'all fire and ice'.[31] As with Welles' stage production, Mankiewicz 'understood the tragedy's message...: Caesar was a Mussolini-like dictator, and Antony his chief factor – A Hitler who realises the fascist dream of his mentor.'[32] Stuart Burge directed another film in 1970, but even the presence of Gielgud (Caesar) and Charlton Heston (Antony) couldn't salvage an obviously cheap and poorly-produced production.

In Stratford-upon-Avon, Anthony Quayle and Michael Langham's 1950 production on an unlocalized stage was fast and efficient: 'John Gielgud as Cassius has never before shown such sustained vehemence... Cassius is beyond question the most important person of every scene in which he figures, even when he is stopping low and looking daggers at great Caesar himself.'[33] The fickleness of the mob was strongly emphasised, but after the tent scene 'the rest is a mopping-up operation of Caesar's ghost, alarms and excursions, and the inevitable falling on antique swords':[34] a regular complaint against productions. Rare praise was reserved for Portia, from whom Gwen Ffrangcon-Davies 'extracts every shade of sympathy and emotion... an exquisite performance, this, sad with a melancholy that achieves a brief and touching beauty',[35] but Quayle's own performance as Antony was 'obliterated' by the mob.

Glen Byam Shaw's 1957 Stratford production was played in togas against a backdrop of pillars. Returning the focus to Brutus, Alec Clunes was a 'liberal idealist all too closely snared by more self-interested conspirators'.[36] Mark Dignam's sardonic Casca, played with 'a neatly calculated edge of rueful self-enjoyment',[37] was singled out for particular praise by all reviewers, the part continuing to stand out; while the interval curtain fell on the image of 'Cinna, the poet, wrongfully stoned to death by the crowd, hanging over the pulpit of the Forum from which Mark Antony has inspired a city's mutiny.'[38]

The play's popularity on foreign stages has taken various forms. In South Africa, following the public assassination of Prime Minister Hendrik Verwoerd in 1960, 'productions of *Julius Caesar* became charged with an increased energy, became, in a sense, symbolic re-enactments of the assassination of Verwoerd, who himself had

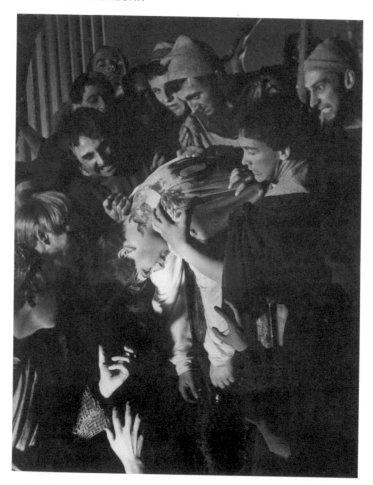

2. Glen Byam Shaw's 1957 Stratford production: 'the interval curtain fell on the image of "Cinna the poet, wrongfully stoned to death by the crowd"'.

come to signify the ideals of Grand Apartheid'.[39] During the apartheid era, productions were generally read as conservative and anti-revolutionary, a demonstration of the penalty for violent uprising. In Munich in 1955, conversely, Fritz Kortner aimed for ambivalent responses: at the moment of assassination, Brutus 'hesitated, and there was a long agonizing pause before "he resolved matters with his stab to the heart"'.[40] Of more interest to Kortner than judgements of 'right' or 'wrong' was the mindless butchery into which the climactic violence descended.

The Shakespeare Festival at Stratford Ontario has produced the play several times. In 1978, an excitingly experimental production by John Wood received rave reviews. Played in brooding darkness, the stage was suddenly illuminated during the assassination: 'so great was the contrast that the white light in which the slaying was bathed seemed blinding and almost obscene . . . the event seemed as ritualized as an act of purification and as appalling as an act of desecration'.[41] The production took the further innovation of removing the mob altogether, leaving Antony alone onstage for a funeral oration that acted as psychological self-exploration. In 1982, Derek Goldby's production 'offended many critics with its harsh violence and its forceful but simplistic treatment of mob psychology'. While individual performances were weak, its 'vision of a system tearing itself apart'[42] was compelling.

Gielgud returned to the role of Caesar for the National Theatre in 1977: 'For once the man dominates, in death as in life: Gielgud suggests both his greatness and why the conspiracy came to a head.'[43] His Ghost hovered over the final proceedings, projecting a spirit of revenge and indomitability. However, the rest of the production failed to impress: Brian Cox's Brutus, whose 'ringing tones betray the unworldly idealism of the born loser',[44] was praised, but the lack of a 'sense of impending, or actual, tyranny' rendered the production 'apolitical' and 'dreary'.[45]

Herbert Wise's 1978 BBC film featured a strong cast including Richard Pasco (Brutus) and Charles Gray (Caesar). Unapologetically Roman in setting, the possibilities of television were utilized to create a conspiratorial atmosphere, particularly in the opening temptation of Brutus: 'We watch Cassius's face past the back of Brutus's head. Until Cassius circles his auditor, we do not know for certain how Brutus is responding. As positions shift, Wise gets an extreme close-up of Brutus's face; we see his eyes as an eyebrow lifts.'[46] A voice-over, meanwhile, betrayed his thoughts only to the audience. The film as a whole, however, felt studio-bound and static.

More recently, a 1999 original-practices experiment at the reconstructed Globe Theatre received mixed reviews: the *Guardian* felt it offered 'no visible interpretation of the play',[47] while the *Telegraph* found it 'comes over with freshness and strength'.[48] The mixed costume (Roman, Elizabethan and modern) served to suggest 'what a live and touchy issue the play's subject – the ethics of tyrannicide – must have been for the original audiences'.[49]

Deborah Warner's 2005 Barbican production hearkened back to earlier spectaculars with a hundred-strong crowd that was particularly praised: 'Head-scarfed and dreadlocked, furious and stunned, surging and chanting behind metal barriers, it gives urgency and variety to a play unappetisingly made up of committee men and soldiers.'[50] Warner's modern-dress production was severe on media-manipulation and public image: Ralph Fiennes' Antony 'gets giddily high on the fans' frenzy',[51] while the Soothsayer was an attention-seeking drunk. In a concurrent production on Broadway directed by Daniel Sullivan, Denzel Washington's Brutus was accused of mangling the verse: 'much of what comes out of his mouth is undifferentiated mush'. He was the star attraction of a 'colourless' Eastern European-set production that compensated for a lack of focus following Caesar's death with 'plenty of plaster-cracking explosions'.[52]

Other twenty-first-century productions have chosen to focus on the conspiracy and intrigue as reflective of modern politics. The intimacy of Bristol's Tobacco Factory allowed Andrew Hilton's 2009 production to be played in near-whispers, and Jacobean cloaks and hats evoked the famous image of the Gunpowder Plot as a key reference point (a costume decision also taken in 1986 by David Thacker's production for the Young Vic), yet the powerful Act 4 scene 1 suggested the callousness of modern bureaucracy as Antony literally signed away his nephew's life. Toneelgroep Amsterdam's 2009 *Roman Tragedies* more explicitly updated Rome to the anonymous 'corridors of power' of modern politics. Here, Renée Fokker's Cassius was a female politician trying to make her way in a man's world, and needed the validation of Roeland Fernhout's Brutus for her coup. Their conflict stemmed from her frustration as Brutus took increasingly more control over 'her' plan; but, in this world, all politicians served their own interests. Across languages, cultures, ideologies and eras, *Julius Caesar* continues to filter commentary on our actions and, more importantly, on what motivates them.

AT THE RSC

Not in Our Stars, but in Ourselves ...

> *Julius Caesar* dramatises issues of enduring relevance – government, dictatorship versus democracy, political assassination, civil war – but not as abstract concepts. Shakespeare presents political action in terms of the human personalities engaged in it.[53]

George Bernard Shaw called *Julius Caesar* 'the most splendidly written political melodrama we possess'. In the twentieth century, what Coleridge 'thought of as the impartiality and evenhandedness of Shakespeare's politics'[54] has been replaced by examinations on the effectiveness of the political assassination of recognizable tyrants. From Hitler and Mussolini to Ceauşescu, the face of twentieth-century fascism has never been far from the thoughts of modern directors. Understandable parallels are there to be drawn. As Fran Thompson, designer of David Thacker's 1993 production at The Other Place, pointed out:

> Written by a comparatively young man at a time of enormous political upheaval, it is a visionary piece of writing pre-empting the English Civil War by almost forty years. Shakespeare's choice of the story of the assassination of Caesar in 44 BC and the subsequent civil war was a vivid metaphor for the struggle to sustain democracy and protect the Republic against a potential dictatorship.[55]

Critics remain largely open to modern dressings for the play, aware of its contemporary relevance, but react badly when a definite place or recognizable tyrant is marked in a production. Referring back to Shakespeare's text, they invariably point out that to equate

Caesar with Hitler or Ceauşescu is to remove the essential ambiguity of the conspirators', and especially Brutus', decision. The more highly praised productions are those whose settings have been 'in no particular time . . . more of a dream [or should we say, nightmare] of fascism'.[56]

Brutus' status as the moral hero of the play has been put into question; Cassius is rarely played now as a machiavellian villain and Antony's motivations have also been severely questioned. Using the scope which Shakespeare's text allows:

> More common now is the approach that equalizes the political forces in the play, emphasizing the many sidedness of each of the major participants. This has . . . to do with an understanding of how Shakespeare's text actually works. Criticism of the play over the past few decades has increasingly revealed the gaps and inconsistencies in these men, the lack of symmetry between private feeling and public posture, the very human muddle that affects their politics. And the theatre has adopted a similar view.[57]

Productions have rarely been able to cope with these modern complexities: 'To reveal itself fully, the play requires an uncut text, fluid stagecraft, and actors of heroic power. And these three factors, sadly enough, have never conjoined.'[58] They may have never conjoined, but the RSC has undoubtedly produced some interesting and exciting productions of *Julius Caesar* which throw light on the political thought and taste of the eras in which they were produced.

By the 1960s, post-war political optimism had been replaced by a growing wave of cynicism. John Blatchley's 1963 production was 'resolutely un-heroic . . . the moral status of all three main characters . . . was diminished as politics was presented as the cynical and self-seeking pursuit of power'.[59]

Setting the predominant mode of design for the play in the productions which followed, the costumes

> pay their tribute to Rome in the toga form of the top dress, but the boots and uniform beneath carry a more universal note. They serve to remind us that tyranny and conspiracy are timeless, as

> also in their drabs and duns they will remind us that war when it comes is conducted in dirt and dust.[60]

Blatchley sought to diminish the epic nature of the play and the almost mythical status of the characters: 'Throughout he sacrifices the atmosphere of an explosive Rome in order to produce a number of petty men groping about on a vast and empty stage.'[61] No heroic shine was placed on Brutus' motives, and it even hinted at moral cowardice in the assassination scene: 'Blatchley also introduced a new conception of the assassination, in which Roy Dotrice as Caesar intentionally threw himself on the sword of Brutus, who was too timid to act.'[62]

This effective piece of staging was adopted in many less cynical productions that followed. With Caesar initiating the final blow that will end his life, his assassination is echoed later in the play by the aided suicides of Cassius and Brutus, giving symmetry to Caesar's revenge:

> Contrasts, even contradictions, are perhaps inevitable in a modern production of *Julius Caesar*. Some aspects of the play, such as political assassination or the claims of democracy versus dictatorship, seem to invite a particularly contemporary staging; but other features, such as belief in auguries, the highly rhetorical style, and especially the presentation of Brutus as an embryonic tragic hero, seem to discourage any specifically contemporary emphasis. Ron Daniels's [1983] production exploited these contrasting elements. In the programme, articles on Roman history and religious beliefs were set against the views of contemporary political figures about 'preventative assassination'.[63]

> On the stage, there was much emphasis on the ceremonial aspect of the 'holy chase' in which Antony takes part and on the ritual laments for the dead Caesar, yet most of the characters wore identical uniforms vaguely reminiscent of *Star Wars*.[64]

The conspirators wore different shades of red, symbolizing empire and blood, but also bringing to mind communist China, or perhaps even the Russian revolution. The contrast between the public and private personas of the characters was given emphasis in this production, which was

> best remembered for presenting Caesar's murder and the major orations in black-and-white, documentary style, on a large television screen lowered to mid-stage. This innovation, intended to highlight the contradictions between public image and private personality in contemporary society, was generally derided as gimmickry by critics and was discontinued later in the season.[65]

However, this was just one element in which Daniels' use of scale and perspective effectively delineated the events and themes of the play:

> Clad in scarlet and gold, [Caesar] and his companions form a line from one side of the stage to the other and advance majestically towards the audience while the organ of Coventry Cathedral blares out in triumphant tones. It is an image from *The Will to Power*,[66] or might be. Riefenstahl's film often used to be cited as an example of the power of the image to persuade the feelings against all sense... The vulgarities of music and design (largely crimson, gold and silver in the first half of the production and very much in the spirit of the Nuremberg rallies) might be intended as a commentary on imperial pretension – do we not have a quotation from Marx in the place of honour in the programme? – but first and foremost they strike one as simply vulgar... There is a complete change of décor for the second half of the play. We are now in *Mother Courage*[67] country, shaggy black carpet underfoot, darkness at the back of the stage, grappling nets hanging from above, and soon, among the half-Roman, half-Hundred Years War military, Mother Courage's cart itself appears, only here it has to serve largely as the body of Brutus's tent. After the pretensions of the first half, men are cut down to size on the battlefield.[68]

Terry Hands is a director keen to remove the political from his productions. In 1987 his production focused on the influence of power in a male-dominated society. He stripped down the stage, using only a textured brick wall onto which images could be projected and effects created with inventive lighting:

> Hands, who likes to light his own shows, creates wonders here. The prodigies of the fatal night conjure up fantastic shapes against the flaring colours of the brick. Shadows mysteriously emerge as from Hades while beams of light spot each of the conspirators in turn.[69]

> His lighting in Julius Caesar is sculptural. It subtly alters the texture and surfaces and manipulates space like a shaping force. This is important, because it underlines what seems to me Hands's main insight into the play. Its first half is mostly bathed in the cold light of public politics. Caesar (David Waller) is an insufferable conviction politician who thrives on exposure. His is a harsh, imperious world: the space is defined by brutal columns of white light which might have been designed by Albert Speer.[70]

> Clearly, there's no alternative to Caesar, and the senators conspire in private darkness; at the end, Brutus and Cassius are isolated in black spaces of error, terror and division pierced by sinister shafts of purple light.[71]

3. Terry Hands' production in 1987 had a stripped down stage and instead used lighting sculpturally. His was 'a harsh imperious world: the space is defined by brutal columns of white light'.

David Thacker's 1993 production at The Other Place was the first RSC production of *Julius Caesar* to dispense with Roman dress. He set his play in a very recognizable European world of late twentieth-century conflict:

> 1989 was a time of huge change in eastern European society. As a revolutionary play *Julius Caesar* sits happily in revolutionary times. We felt that the political schism in the Eastern Bloc which is so fresh in our minds would give the production dynamism and contemporary relevance...We agreed there was little to be gained from squeezing the play into a specifically Romanian, Russian or Czechoslovakian setting or by saying that Caesar is Gorbachev, Ceauşescu, Honecker. We were not wanting to create direct or specific parallels but rather to draw on the power of contemporary political change in order to demonstrate the seriousness and relevance of the issues addressed in the play. To be non-specific about a setting is not to be evasive or indecisive but to allow members of the audience to make other associations of dictatorship and the struggle for democracy for instance in South Africa or Latin America.

> The potency of modern dress cannot be underestimated for an audience which might find Shakespeare's verse alienating. Images of suited politicians and uniformed generals in contrast to a poorly dressed crowd have the immediacy and apparent veracity of a news story on television. The struggle for democracy encapsulated in *Julius Caesar* is sadly still going on.[72]

In order to hit home the contemporary experience and make the audience more directly involved with the action of the play, Thacker decided to stage the play as a promenade production. The audience stood around the actors, witnesses to the action at close proximity. One reviewer commented:

> To find yourself standing a mere yard from the assassins as they roll up their shirt-sleeves and bathe their arms in Caesar's blood is as nicely horrid as you can imagine.[73]

In an interview for the *Independent*, Thacker explained his choice:

> This is a play about people manipulating or dealing with crowds...I thought it would be theatrically exciting to have people there on stage so they experience being in a large group of people hearing the speeches. I hope it might make them think 'Would I believe this?' in a more concrete way than usual.[74]

A fine balance was reached in which the audience were not compelled to engage with the actors but were used as an integral part of the staging:

> To call this production promenade is only a short hand to say there are no seats: this is not a conventional audience-stage relationship. A promenade performance usually means moving from area to area in a huge space so that the audience is literally taken on a journey. This production is, in reality, more 'environmental'. The audience is in and of that environment,

4. David Thacker's 1993 RSC production had a promenade audience: 'To find yourself standing a mere yard from the assassins as they roll up their shirt-sleeves and bathe their arms in Caesar's blood is as nicely horrid as you can imagine.'

not only close to but also participating in the action: the human walls in which our drama is played.[75]

In creating a direct correlation between what people were witnessing on the television at home sitting on their sofa, and what they saw standing in the theatre, Thacker took his audiences into a world disturbingly reminiscent of the Bosnian conflict. The battles took place amidst the sound of machine-gun fire, and propagandists walked in among the audience and actors with video cameras filming the action. This method of staging gave the production an energy and excitement many others have lacked. Many praised the production's contemporary directness:

> Photos of David Sumner's Caesar festoon the theatre walls, and then on comes the man himself, tracked by a video-camera as he saunters through the modern-day mob in his expensive Italian serge . . . The lynching of Cinna the poet might be the climax of an ugly riot on a London estate. Philippi might be happening in Bosnia tomorrow. This is not a *Julius Caesar* for those in search of subtlety; but for those who want action, it is a production to admire.[76]

The stage devices, which had proved effective in Thacker's production, were picked up in David Farr's touring production in 2004:

> Stage managers double as performers, visibly pushing computer keys to make the neon lights fizz and flash for a Roman storm, then playing servants, then crouching down with follow-spots that irradiate Brutus's face or video cameras that transpose public speeches to a screen behind an empty stage. Empty that is, except when battle occurs – and institutional chairs and tables are hurled about or used as barricades.[77]

Although the design had references to conflict in Eastern Europe, and especially civil conflict in Russia, the inferences reflected current feelings about the war in Iraq:

> Together with designer Ti Green, he has created a loosely contemporary Rome that describes the confused world we live in

at the moment, one in which people want their leaders to be strong and yet not arrogantly autocratic, and where a clear-cut objective – to remove a tyrant in the name of freedom – unleashes violent disorder. The mob – dressed in fashionable casuals – clamber up steel gantries, holler the name 'Caesar' and unfurl banners onto which video images of the suited politician are projected.[78]

the programme is filled with references to Putin and Berlusconi... when Brutus urges the assassination of Caesar, even if 'the quarrel will bear no colour for the thing he is', we suddenly seem to be in the chilling world of pre-emptive regime-change.[79]

For Always I am Caesar

Caesar's weaknesses, and there are many, balance but do not cancel out his symbolic strength.[80]

Contrary to what many critics assume, *Julius Caesar* is not a play of two halves. The action is continuous and is often best when played without an interval. When a break is taken after the assassination scene, or the murder of Cinna the Poet, it can often kill the momentum of the proceeding acts and give the play a disjointed feel. Directors are keen to establish a strong sense of Caesar's influence and dominant spirit after the assassination by use of various stage devices. In 1968, director John Barton knew

that Caesar never ceases to rule. In death his presence governs the tragedy[81]... In life, in the person of Brewster Mason, the dictator is physically dominating, not the husk we have had so often. On the very edge of death, bleeding from the daggers of the faction, he advances upon the agonized Brutus like the incarnation of doom itself, and at '*Et tu, Brute?*— Then fall, Caesar' [3.1.84], himself guides home the blade.

From that moment Brutus is lost. From that minute the leaders of the conspiracy are haunted men. Caesar is in his coffin, but the mantle he first wore on a summer's evening in his tent, 'That day he overcame the Nervii' [3.2.184], is used, tattered now and bloodstained, as the symbol of his avengers. During the parley upon the plains of Philippi the rebels see the sign before them. At the last, battle done, Mark Antony, even in his salute to the 'noblest Roman of them all' covers Brutus's body with the mantle in which... Caesar had fallen at the base of Pompey's statue. Moreover, Mr Barton lets the ghost of Caesar walk abroad. He appears not only at Sardis, but he comes also, a figure barely seen in the gloom, after the parting of Brutus and Cassius before battle. Later, in his moment of suicide, Brutus falls dead while the silent apparition towers above him.[82]

In 1972, Mark Dignam played Caesar as a genuinely dangerous figure. The set and costuming heavily featured fascist symbolism, with red, white and black the predominant colours:

It is full of banners, insignia of Caesar and arrogant legionaries within whose hearing it's safer to keep silence, and almost literally bestridden by a colossus. Mark Dignam is a formidable Caesar, bland, brazen and imperious as he strides downstage on his red carpet to outstare gods and Gods alike, a half-smile, half-scowl on a face alarmingly like that of a 60 year old Mussolini. Indeed, both he and Rome itself might have been lifted from one of the Duce's more vain-glorious fantasies, down to the scampering retinue of sycophantic senators who chorus 'hail Caesar' whenever his voice hits that public, finite note which they know to be their cue...[83]

Trevor Nunn had an immense statue of this 'colossus of Rome' permanently on stage to symbolize Caesar's dominating spirit:

Critics admired Dignam's performance and praised the production's overall emphasis on Caesar. The nearly continuous presence on stage of a huge statue of Caesar underscored the character's dominance as a public figure and, after his death, his undiminished influence on events.[84]

5. Trevor Nunn's 1972 RSC production was 'full of banners, insignia of Caesar'; 'Mark Dignam is a formidable Caesar, bland, brazen and imperious as he strides downstage on his red carpet to outstare gods and Gods alike, a half-smile, half-scowl on a face alarmingly like that of a 60 year old Mussolini.'

The statue was also a potent reminder of how Caesar's own persona had been enveloped by a public myth:

> There you have the man whose public image has so engulfed the private person that personal relationships are no longer comfortable. The same dichotomy was in this production well conveyed by the introduction of Caesar's colossal statue into the one scene of his domestic life. Standing uneasily in the shadow of his public image Caesar cannot act naturally to his friends or

even to his wife . . . The most significant irony of the play is that Brutus, regretting that in order to destroy the public Caesar he must kill the private one, ends by recognising that although the private friend has been duly killed, the public Caesar persists indestructibly. This is the lesson repeatedly voiced by the characters and embodied in the visitation of Caesar's spirit to Brutus's tent on the night before the conspirators are finally liquidated at Philippi. For this visitation the statue, terrifyingly heralded by the nightmare cries of the sleepers, served well . . . [85]

In the working out of Caesar's revenge, supernatural and well as symbolic inferences were also placed on the statue: 'Even after his death his gargantuan statue looms above the action, the features lit by a symbolic red spot as one by one his enemies perish.'[86]

Many productions have been more visceral in their depiction of Caesar's influence after death. In 1987 his reanimated corpse was seen on the battlefield:

The ghost of Caesar, as promised in the tent scene, reappears at Philippi walking slowly among Brutus's forces and forcing him to back stage left in horror. When Brutus finally runs onto the sword held by Strato kneeling on the edge of the stage with his back to the audience, the triumphant ghost begins to march down centre stage slowly.[87]

More chillingly, in David Thacker's 1993 production one of the soldiers killing prisoners after the battle removes his balaclava and reveals himself to Brutus as the Ghost of Caesar.[88]

'The Work We Have in Hand, Most Bloody, Fiery, and Most Terrible'

Every decade has its despots and you always wonder how did society fall for these people and obey them. But *Julius Caesar* is about more than that. It is a play about power and what happens if that power is toppled. It looks at what happens if you kill a leader. It is very easy to say we should assassinate Hitler or Saddam Hussein but what does that unleash?[89]

As we know, regime change can unleash violence, hatred and extremism. If, as Brutus says, 'there is a tide in the affairs of man', one must question if he has chosen his time wisely. Regardless of his underestimation of Antony, behind the conspiracy and plot, which is executed in the rational world, there lies a supernatural inevitability in the working out of fate. Even Cassius towards the end of the play questions his edict that it is 'not in our stars, but in ourselves' that we are thus. Tragically, Brutus' vision of the purification of Rome by ritual bloodletting, a role enacted by his ancestors, has the adverse effect – a 'vile contagion' follows which will destroy Rome and all that he lives for:

> By the end of the play, Brutus has killed all those he loves. He kills Caesar and he kills his wife and Cassius, by his behaviour on the battlefield which brings about the defeat of the army. It is a very much more mysterious play than is often assumed. What about the soothsayer, whom Caesar hears above the hubbub and din of the crowd, the question of the barrenness of Caesar's wife, her dreams of Caesar's statue spouting blood, the ghosts, the suicides, the portents, the mob which tears to pieces a man who coincidentally bears a conspirator's name? Is this about anything as banal as politics? We are talking about a lurid and very romantic study of the effects of passion in a male-dominated world.
>
> Then again, the ghost of Caesar describes himself as Brutus's 'evil spirit'. Why does he not say that he is the ghost of Caesar? We can speculate as to what he means by Brutus's evil spirit. Is it Brutus's ability to kill the things he loves?[90]

Is Brutus' act like Macbeth's? Was Caesar destined to be king and has Brutus usurped divine right and committed a sacrilegious act by his murder? There are similarities but, unlike Macbeth, we cannot call Brutus a villain as his intents are for Rome and the ideals it signifies. However, the effectiveness of Shakespeare's writing of the assassination scene, in which an all-too-mortal and defenceless man is brutally stabbed in front of our eyes, cannot help but make our attitude ambivalent to the conspirators' actions. The similarities lie in what 'regicide' unleashes, and this has become a major concern of the modern director. Could the conspirators ever succeed with such a murder on their hands and conscience? In the last fifty years there has been increased savagery in the depiction of violence and the use of blood as the major symbol of the play's thematic concerns. From a play that was considered Stoic and wordy, *Julius Caesar* has progressed into something much more visceral. In 1991 Steven Pimlott's production paid service to modern and recognizable depictions of physical horror:

> Pimlott appears to have a real relish for violence. The show memorably captures the baying, brainless belligerence of the mob, and the scene in which they lay into the gentle poet Cinna is almost unwatchable in its sadistic ferocity. And, far from carving Caesar as a dish fit for the gods, the assassination is lingeringly, almost longingly presented like a scene in a 'slasher' horror movie, with lashings of blood with which the conspirators smear their faces as well as their hands.[91]

The play's obsession with methods of suicide and slow inflictions of death has never been so marked. Caesar's extended knifing is a messy kill at the bullfight. Cinna the Poet is torn to pieces together with his verses. The architectural corridor of Rome is replaced in a long interval by the sarcophagus of Sardis and Philippi. Here soldiers lie down and cringe in trench helmets like frozen figures in a First World War memorial sculpture.[92]

Taken to another level of experience,

> David Thacker's presentation of the assassination scene made the audience feel uncomfortably close to the action. The conspirators ominously emerged from the audience one by one and in a trance-like series of moves advanced towards Caesar and stabbed him. Caesar who was reduced to his knees finally grabbed Brutus by the legs and looked into his eyes before uttering '*Et tu, Brute?*'. All of the conspirators avoided making eye contact with the audience in the moments after, as Caesar's body was wheeled out on a hospital trolley.[93]

Peter Hall's 1995 production was not well received but was particularly noted for the fact that:

> Visible blood provided a recurring motif: it spurted from the joint between Caesar's neck and shoulder after Casca stabbed him; there was plentiful blood on the hands and swords of the conspirators after the assassination; it spurted from Cinna the Poet after the mob had stabbed and beaten him to death; a bucket of blood was poured down the steps after the mob scene; Caesar's corpse, on display, was stained red with blood; Octavius's face, in battle was streaked with blood; blood streamed down the face of the vast effigy of Caesar at the end of the play.[94]

The stage became a nightmarish place of paranoia and disorder, in which an uncanny atmosphere foreboded the imminent threat of physical violence:

> Hall's initial achievement is to evoke a Rome in the throes of a living nightmare. John Gunter's sombre, panelled set is dominated by a giant mask of Caesar, Guy Woolfenden's eerie chords fill the air with a sense of omen, and public figures are beset by private fears. Christopher Benjamin's Caesar starts nervously on being accosted by a soothsayer, and John Nettles's Brutus gazes into the sultry pit where the feast of Lupercal is taking place with the horror of a man witnessing the birth of a dictatorship.[95]

In Edward Hall's production in 2000, the removal of Caesar was equated with the removal of Rome's heart and the slow death of the body politic:

> Hall made some extraordinary decisions ... omitting the first scene of tribunes and plebeians altogether, replacing it with an initial tableau in which a reappearing ragged Soothsayer opens a small trap on the forestage to take out and display aloft a bleeding heart, presumably the 'heart within the beast' [2.2.42] which augurers could not find for Caesar. Later, hung upside down in chains, Cinna the poet's heart is plucked from his breast by a terrifying Brünhilde[96] figure – apparently the same who has led

Caesar in procession onto the stage at the start of act 1, scene 2, with a rousing, sung anthem to the 'Res-publica'...in this production, woman as Fascist functionary come into her own, on terms of complete equality to her male counterparts.

...the battles as such never took place and there was no fighting. There was some marching under falling snow, some thumping on the earth with staves, spears, or pikes, until the victims of a battle taking place elsewhere stumbled and staggered in, crumpling to the ground – to the accompaniment of another sung Latin dirge – smearing the walls with their blood.[97]

In this production the formation of a uniformed and well-organized militia made up from Caesar's entourage took the place of the traditional mob. At Antony's oration they infiltrated the audience, shouting inflammatory remarks as Tom Mannion's manipulative Antony whipped them up into frenzy of hate, ready to exact his revenge. Many critics decried the fact that an essential element of the play was missing by the omission of the ordinary Roman plebeians. Indeed, there does not appear to be a production of *Julius Caesar* in which the handling of the mob has been universally praised:

The citizens of Rome have a corporate identity in *Julius Caesar* that makes them as vital an element as any one of the leading characters of the drama. And the director who can't manage them effectively can't manage the play either. There are a number of alternatives, of course. You may use a large body of actors on zigger zagger lines and make your points by sheer weight of numbers. Or you may go to the opposite extreme and banish the crowd to the wings or even the audience. Or you may go in for a Brecht-like stylisation where a small group of actors is confined into a tiny space thereby suggesting by means of hemming in a small group an immensely larger one.[98]

This is all very well in theory but in practice these options, tried in their various forms have failed to impress: large crowds of extras have led to excessive 'rhubarbing', and when played by amateur actors, have not provided the emotional response required; the mob have been dispensed with altogether and replaced by sound systems offstage; and the audience itself has been forced into that uncomfortable role, unsure of the levels of participation expected.

That ordinary citizens should be the ones who are manipulated into acts of extreme violence and civil decent is an element of horror essential to the play. Violence leads to more violence, and Antony, possessed by the tyrannical spirit of Caesar, utters one of the most chilling speeches in Shakespeare's canon:

> And Caesar's spirit, ranging for revenge,
> With Ate by his side, come hot from hell,
> Shall in these confines with a monarch's voice
> Cry havoc and let slip the dogs of war,
> That this foul deed shall smell above the earth
> With carrion men, groaning for burial. (3.1.289–94)

... the chilling incantation of any extremist given the motive and the opportunity to mobilise ordinary people with petty hatreds and self-serving motives into violent expression.

THE DIRECTORS CUT: INTERVIEWS WITH EDWARD HALL, DAVID FARR AND LUCY BAILEY

Edward Hall, son of the RSC's founder Sir Peter Hall, was born in 1967 and trained at Leeds University and the Mountview Theatre School before cutting his teeth at the Watermill Theatre in the 1990s. His first Shakespearean success was a production of *Othello* in 1995, though he used the experience as inspiration to found Propeller, an all-male theatre company with whom he directed *The Comedy of Errors* and *Henry V*, which ran together in repertory during the 1997–98 season, and *Twelfth Night* in 1999, all at the Watermill. In 1998 he made his directorial debut with the RSC on a production of *The Two Gentlemen of Verona*, and would go on to work again with the company on *Henry V* in 2000–01 and, in the 2001–02 season, the production of *Julius Caesar* which he will be discussing here. In between *Henry* and *Caesar* that year, Hall returned to the Watermill to direct *Rose Rage*, his (in)famous and celebrated abattoir-set adaptation of the *Henry VI* trilogy. He left the

RSC for good in 2002 and has continued to work with Propeller on such productions as *A Midsummer Night's Dream* in 2003 and *Twelfth Night* and *The Taming of the Shrew* in 2007. He became Artistic Director of Hampstead Theatre in 2010.

David Farr is a writer and director, and has had an extraordinarily prolific career for such a young talent. He was Artistic Director of the Gate Theatre, London, from 1995 to 1998, moving on to the position of Joint Artistic Director of Bristol Old Vic from 2002 to 2005. He became Artistic Director of the Lyric Theatre Hammersmith in 2005, where his productions included *Water*, *The Resistible Rise of Arturo Ui*, *The Birthday Party*, *The Magic Carpet*, *Ramayana*, *The Odyssey* and a new version of Kafka's *Metamorphosis*. As a playwright, his work includes *The Nativity*, *Elton John's Glasses* and *Crime and Punishment in Dalston*. David joined the RSC as an Associate Director in 2009, since which time he has directed Greg Hicks as Leontes in *The Winter's Tale* (2009) and as the title role in *King Lear* (2010), though his first work with the company came in between his tenures at the Gate and the Old Vic, writing *Night of the Soul* for the company, which was produced at the Pit Theatre in 2001. He returned to direct an award-winning production of *Coriolanus* (also starring Greg Hicks) in 2002, and a boldly modernist production of *Julius Caesar* at the Swan Theatre in 2004, which David revived in his first season at Lyric Hammersmith.

Lucy Bailey started her directorial career in experimental theatre and moved on to work in opera before returning to theatre in the mid-1990s. She continued her musical affiliations, however, founding the Gogmagogs in 1995 with violinist Nell Catchpole, known for their exciting hybrid performances combining virtuoso string playing and experimental physical theatre. Her breakthrough 1999 production of Tennessee Williams' *Baby Doll* in Birmingham found critical acclaim, and transferred to the National and the West End. Other directorial credits include *Lady from the Far Sea* for the Birmingham Repertory Theatre, *Glass Eels* and *Comfort Me with Apples* for Hampstead Theatre, and *Don't Look Now* for the Lyceum Theatre in Sheffield and the Lyric Hammersmith. Her first major work with Shakespeare came in 2006 in her production of *Titus Andronicus* at Shakespeare's Globe, followed by productions of *Timon of Athens* in 2008, and *Macbeth* in 2010. Her 2009–10 production of *Julius Caesar* for the RSC marked her directorial debut with the company.

Why is the play called *Julius Caesar* when he dies halfway through the play?

EH: I suppose he would have had a lot of trouble on his hands trying to call it *Brutus*, *Cassius* or *Antony*, because they are all pretty big parts and all three actors would probably want billing! I think because Julius Caesar was the centre of that universe and the play is about whether or not the conspirators should topple it. He is a huge figure, and one I think Shakespeare was fascinated by. I think he was fascinated by all the lives of Plutarch, and particularly Julius Caesar. My production started with the triumph and I think that and the title help to show that this man is as close to a king, an emperor, even a god, as somebody could get to within a republic.

You have to remember that the Elizabethan audience did not live in a republic; Shakespeare is writing a play about a completely different political system and in many respects is exploring a theme, which he carried on to explore in *Macbeth*: the divine right of kings. When is it your duty to stand up and rebel against order and authority? It's a constant debate of our time. If 300,000 people march in the street against the war in Iraq and Tony Blair ignores them, what else do we do? Shakespeare is exploring that idea but set in a period removed from the one in which he was living to avoid any danger involved in depicting the overthrow of a ruler; famously, the deposition scene was cut from *Richard II*, and then performed at the Globe on the eve of Essex's revolt against Elizabeth I. Any stories on stage that depicted a ruler having their authority challenged were very difficult to get past the censor. *Julius Caesar* gave Shakespeare a great canvas to paint on where he could explore these issues fully. He touched on these themes lightly in *Macbeth*, where he couldn't quite be as explicit as I think he wanted to be because he was writing for James I, a monarch who believed absolutely in the divine right of the king. So I think he called this

Roman play *Julius Caesar* to make it absolutely clear that this was the story that he was exploring, and that it had no bearing on his present political or social circumstances: it was to take the heat off.

DF: The play is fundamentally about what happens when you remove a king, or what happens when you remove a man of power who tries to reach too far, so the shadow of him hangs over the whole political system afterwards. Although I suppose Brutus is technically the lead character, he is in no sense in the same way that Hamlet or King Lear is. The play examines the whole political structure and the effect that the death of the king has, so that is probably the reason for the title. For me the play is a wonderful, modern, pertinent examination of the tendency for a leader to try and push just a bit too far, in terms of their status within a society. That could be Elizabeth I or Vladimir Putin or Berlusconi in the modern world; we see it happen again and again and again. I remember when I directed it we discussed a lot the way in which modern leaders pass various laws: immunity from prosecution is a good example, which Putin and Berlusconi both passed, or whether it be certain presidential decrees, like George W. Bush's creation of a particular department answerable only to him in order that he could bypass certain areas of the Pentagon. There are many wonderful modern examples of what Caesar has done in claiming his crown.

LB: It's clear when you watch the play that the greatest man on that stage is Julius Caesar. Once he has been assassinated it feels as if all the rest are pygmies compared to him. He dominates the first half of the play, as the charismatic, verging on despotic, leader, and after he has been killed he returns to haunt it. I felt that the unifying element to the play was Julius Caesar – far from leaving the play, as soon as he is killed, his spirit lives on – no one stops talking about him. He returns in the second half to haunt Brutus, and in our production he appears at the very end as the revenging ghost stalking the battlefield, taking Brutus with him. One of the central questions that preoccupied Shakespeare and his contemporary audience was the nature of monarchy – at what point does monarchy become tyranny? Is it possible to rule without resorting to violence and suppression? Is assassination ever justified and does it produce change for the better? *Julius Caesar* reads like a political thriller, all the action of the first half is the tense lead-up to the assassination, and then the second half is the bloody aftermath. One man's blood becomes a sea of blood.

Did you opt for an ancient setting or something to suggest more modern parallels?

EH: My production had a more contemporary setting. It had an aura of fascism about it. I took the slogan 'Peace, Freedom and Liberty', which is one of the slogans which comes up in the play, as the party's slogan: that's what Caesar stood for. We had a huge neon sign at the back that lit up during the opening procession and the climax saying 'Peace, Freedom and Liberty'. There were dark uniforms and jackboots, but over the top of that there was the stencil of ancient Rome: people wore rather elegant togas so you could still feel the classical world on stage.

6. Edward Hall's contemporary setting, RSC 2001–02: 'We had a huge neon sign at the back which lit up during the opening procession and the climax saying "Peace, Freedom and Liberty". There were dark uniforms and jackboots but over the top of that there was the stencil of ancient Rome.'

DF: We had a strong modern setting. We had a clear idea in our heads, which we didn't need the audience to fully understand in order to experience the story, but which we essentially created in our heads: a modern nation state in which a Putin-like leader was doing exactly this, was attempting to extend his role into a long-term presidential role. At the time we were doing it Putin was considering changing the constitution from a five-year presidential reign to a ten-year one. He didn't do it in the end, but he was considering it and we were inspired by that. So we used a modern language and we explored the idea of a theatre company invading an existing government space, a factory I suppose, in order to present a kind of guerrilla underground version of this play as a mode of protest. There was a whole Brechtian guerrilla theatre quality. The audience weren't in on that and we didn't try and make it overt, it was a way in which to make the story clear and feel urgent and immediate. It is a short play and it has got an intense pace about it; it doesn't have as much eccentricity as some of Shakespeare's other plays, it just does exactly what is intended, like a thriller. I was making it for the regional tour and I had a strong desire to make it for what I perceived to be a young audience, or an audience that was new to Shakespeare, and I felt it was important to make, in a sophisticated way, the work feel urgent and contemporary.

LB: I was immediately drawn to the primal brutal world that Shakespeare depicts in this play, but at the same time very conscious of its contemporary resonance. It describes a world where the decisions of a few powerful men affect the lives of hundreds and thousands – where the repercussions of these decisions end up in mass slaughter. It couldn't be more relevant today. The belief system of this world is pre-Christian, based on the amoral activities of the god dictated by signs and portents. A world of stunning creativity and unbelievable cruelty – and not so far from our post-Christian world, which has returned to an excessive and similar obsession with sex and violence.

Working with my designer Bill Dudley, our first instinct was to avoid any architectural representation of Rome on stage. We wanted to capture the atmosphere of violence and panic that is the backdrop to the play – and is the climate in which the assassination takes place. This led us to the use of film to suggest a Rome full of frightened people – an irrational, unstable world governed by portents and dreams. Our set was incredibly simple to look at, but hard to realize. A series of six gauzes which could move in parallel to each other, creating entrances between them or becoming one flat back drop. On to these gauzes we projected images of our cast duplicated to become a massive crowd. These films would echo the action on stage, lending every scene in the first half a sense of frenetic movement and panic, and in the second half capturing the vast military campaign.

Do audiences need to be familiar with the back-story/events leading up to the play before it begins?

EH: No, I don't think an audience should ever need to be familiar with any of that. I think it's our job to deliver the play in such a way that somebody can walk in from a heavy day's work, collapse in a seat, look up and get taken on a journey where they don't have to have swallowed a book or a dictionary to understand what is going on.

LB: It's a brilliantly written political thriller – a real page-turner. The play starts mid-crisis, at fever pitch and continues at that pace, never letting up. Shakespeare is brilliant at encapsulating what has gone on before with an amazing brevity and speed. I think the challenge to the stage director is to tell the story in a way that illuminates the text. All the information you need is there in Shakespeare's words, so it's up to the production to excavate it. In the opening scene the Tribunes berate the crowd for forgetting their loyalty to their beloved Pompey, and cheering Caesar who destroyed him. I chose to extend the opening, fleshing out what Shakespeare has cleverly depicted in words with a more visceral stage picture. The Lupercal is a fertility festival and has its roots in the legend of Romulus and Remus and the violent birth of Rome. It is being celebrated in Rome on the same day as Caesar's triumph. Caesar knows his victory over Pompey's sons is extremely unpopular so he cannily turns it into a popular triumph by hijacking the Lupercal Carnival. This is implied rather than stated by Shakespeare. So we staged an amazing Bacchanalian and violent Lupercal with the wolfmen whipping women and segued deftly into Caesar's magnificent triumph, the same confetti and madness in the air as affected the carnival, underlining the political manoeuvring of this ruthless man.

DF: Not at all. There are two things which you have to make clear. One is the notion of what a Lupercal holiday is – that is a difficult thing – and more important and equally difficult, because it is only related and not shown on stage, is the ceremony of the turning down of the Crown: something that can be difficult for an audience to fully grasp. But once those two things are grasped, and if you can clarify exactly what they mean in your production, then the piece becomes crystal clear after that. Interestingly, I found in a contemporary setting the second half to be much easier, because I felt the whole notion of it breaking into civil war and the modernity of warfare very familiar. In the negotiating scene which goes wrong in the second half we used United Nations' language, and suddenly the whole thing became alive and I found what everyone says is difficult about the play in the second half to be extremely rewarding.

What I found more difficult were Lupercalian celebrations and the sort of astrological chaos of the first few scenes, where they are talking about lions and that whole more cosmic Roman area. We explored that in a psyche-of-the-country kind of way and that worked to an extent, but as always with Shakespeare he was writing historical plays for his time. The difficulty this creates when directing is the overwhelming impulse to make it immediate for our time, but of course Shakespeare didn't write for our time, he wrote for his time and so there is always a tension – a very interesting tension – that you do not want to just sit them back in the period, because he wasn't interested in that. But at the same time, if you modernize thoughtlessly you are going to come a cropper, because he wasn't writing for the year 2000.

And what about the specifically Roman stuff, such as Brutus adhering to the Stoic philosophy and Cassius to the Epicurean? Shakespeare must have expected most of his audience to know what he was talking about, but most of our audiences don't have a clue, not having studied classics in school as every educated male did in Shakespeare's time.

EH: I don't think that's true. I think the majority of Shakespeare's audience had no idea what these forms of rhetoric or belief were: most of the people who watched his plays were illiterate. The small amount of people who usually paid for the writing and performing of the plays would have understood that, but where Shakespeare is so brilliant is that you do not have to know any of these things to appreciate that one man is a jealous bear looking for revenge, and another man is torn so terribly because he has the ultimate liberal intellect and he understands every single angle of an argument. In a way that is Brutus's curse. Stoicism can be confused with feeling relaxed about everything, and it's not, and I think it drives Brutus into such a knot that his wife famously mutilates herself because she can't bear the tension that he seems to be under. I don't think you have to know anything about Stoicism or Epicureanism or any of those things to understand that. I think it's an interesting sideline if you want to study more and I think it's great for academics to expostulate on, but fundamentally it's not something that drove us in the rehearsal room. What Shakespeare has written is a very strong, defined character and the lines and the action are an expression of his character and not of an intellectual idea. It may be that when you look back on it you say Brutus is a Stoic. But Brutus wouldn't necessarily say he was a Stoic, and you don't need to understand what Stoicism is to play Brutus. In fact it can be a hindrance that overtakes the role.

DF: But that translates beautifully into modern ideas of pacifism and activism. Those ideas are timeless. The language in which they are couched might be unfamiliar, but you are not trying to give the audience a lesson in stoic philosophy and the ideas are crystal clear: the notion of patient acceptance of faith against those notions of fighting faith, and self-determination. Cassius is a phenomenally modern character. Brutus is difficult because he is a less modern character, but I look at someone like Barack Obama and think in a funny way Brutus is coming back in: the emphasis on moral centre, on rhetoric, has actually returned after a period in which I feel politics was very much about delivery and about making the correct decision under pressure, and not really about ideology and morality. We seem now to be returning to these areas, so that debate is still alive now. I found the debate between Cassius and Brutus to be particularly sensitive: the most alive material that we dealt with.

How did you stage the assassination itself?

EH: One of the big problems with the play is blood: there's an awful lot of it and once it gets on the stage, from a practical point of view it gets very sticky. And I wanted a lot of blood. There's blood on people's hands, they talk about the blood and how you can smell it; it's very, very important, especially for what happens afterwards. I had Caesar in his chair and there was a very white, perspex sheet that the chair was on that went up the back of the RST and up into the fly floor with a picture of Caesar on it. It was like a beautiful big piece of scenery, but when he was murdered we could chuck blood all over it, because we then dropped it from the fly floor and dragged it off stage and all the blood was gone when we wanted it to be. It was very violent and very bloody and you saw that he ended up being stabbed again and again and again, and everybody had to have a hand in it. It was violent, sodden and very bloody.

DF: The murder was brutal and dirty and messy and, very much because of the costumes, the men in suits, and the sense that Caesar was clearly conducting some kind of high-level cabinet meeting, it felt political and it took place in real life. I was looking for a level of ritual as well, when they dip their hands in the blood of Caesar. The blood was not naturalistic because the whole play was not presented in that naturalistic way: there was a bucket of blood brought on and there was a strange ritualistic quality to that which counterpointed the more grubby realism of the actual killing. Because there was so much blood people could dip their hands in, and this emphasized the sacrificial quality of the killing, which was very effective.

LB: Our one piece of physical set was the plinth that Caesar ascends just before his assassination. It looked like a slab of marble fit for slaughter. Our idea was that the assassins would appear like wolves from the dark and leap onto the plinth. Caesar fights back with amazing ferocity. Greg Hicks, who acted Caesar, made this moment very believable – being lithe and athletic. The grand historical assassination that the conspirators imagined degenerates into frantic butchery. Brutus waits for an opportunity to kill him in a memorable and meaningful way, but finally scrabbles up the steps, pushing the manic killers aside, and grabs the body from them. The moment is not heroic, just ghastly.

How, with a limited number of actors, did you go about creating the mob scenes?

EH: We put the actors all over the theatre. I personally can't imagine that scene being done any other way than using your audience as the crowd, and I am sure that's what would have happened when Shakespeare did it; several hundred people hopefully (unless it's a Tuesday matinee!), and you get them for free. So we had actors out in the audience at different points shouting and jeering. The audience weren't invited to join in – because why would they? – but they certainly enabled the rebels and Antony to directly address the audience with the corpse of Caesar, and talk to those various different actors dotted around the building. They were positioned up in the gallery and would shout down at the stage. They had iron bars, which they banged on bits of the auditorium – I think we damaged the poor old RST at some point – and then we had one of the crowd come in on a rope and abseil down from the balcony into the stalls as the mob made their way onto stage. It was a scene that we played directly out to the audience.

DF: We started the play with every single actor charging onto the stage and setting the play up, bringing lights, video, etc., and then at the end of that sequence they were all able to leap onto the walls of this factory structure. With the exception of the two Tribunes, every single person, including the actors who played Brutus, Cassius, Antony and Caesar, were the crowd. In a sense it was a Brechtian technique: you play those twenty people and there was no illusion of any kind that it was real. I can't stand it when theatre tries to pretend that nine people are a hundred in a naturalistic sense. There was a clear filmic way in which that scene was created, and if theatre accepts the artifice then the audience are willing to understand. It's about highlighting and accepting the artifice.

LB: *Julius Caesar* is a great ensemble piece as the plebs have such an important role. The first half of the play is predominantly a discussion between the people that rule and the people that are ruled, and it's how you represent the people that are ruled that's most tricky. I worked very closely with my choreographer and fight director to create a stage and film language for these crowds, mobs, and armies. A huge part of our work with the ensemble has concentrated on creating an expressionistic gestural world to capture the panic and hysteria that is unleashed in the play.

We filmed our cast and kept multiplying them, so that our group of actors could become a huge crowd. I think the template for the filming was based on two ideas provided by Bill [Dudley – designer]. The Elgin Marbles and Trajan's Column, which depicts scenes commemorating the Emperor Trajan's victories, fascinated him. It's very sophisticated in the way it captures complex scenes with only a couple of centimetres of relief – it is like the very first graphic novel, or newsreel. This two-dimensional language became the main inspiration for the filming technique, alongside the work of the photographer Eadweard Muybridge. He took a series of pictures that analysed the human body, how the muscles and limbs behaved, capturing every stage of the process. What we liked, which wouldn't necessarily have occurred to Muybridge, was the heroic aspect of it. The men and women he captured repeating everyday actions became epic and strangely moving. I went to see the Elgin Marbles at the British Museum with Fotini Dimou, my costume designer. The depictions of these warriors, caught in violent images of killing and dying, also informed our approach to the armies and battles that are such a huge and difficult part of the play. We were really impressed by the athleticism of these Elgin warriors: semi-naked, very vulnerable, but powerful expressions of the sheer beauty of the human body.

And how did you tackle the 'big speeches', such as Mark Antony's oration? It must be tough to make words that are so familiar seem new.

EH: I think that is one of the traps with Shakespeare; you think that everyone knows bits really well. You just have to leave that outside the door. Those famous speeches have become famous in themselves, but people forget what's before and what's after, and largely, if you get the play right, you just arrive at those moments. Tom Mannion is such an extraordinary wordsman, he was so calm and charismatic and clear, he played out the action of trying to persuade the audience to tell him what they thought so well, that I think we just approached it as you would any other scene. The action in that speech for the actor playing Antony is to try and get to a point where the crowd do what you want them to do. You can't do that by telling them; you can only do that by reasoning with them. I think it would have been an extremely popular and interesting scene for the audience of the day to watch, because I think the groundlings would have liked to think of themselves as being politically active. In *Richard III* there is a whole scene with the crowd and the Mayor of London where the citizens of London are needed by Richard to pull off his coup. He illustrates the power of the people again in *Henry VI* in Cade's revolt.

In *Caesar* Shakespeare writes a scene where Antony harnesses the energy of the mob and shows how manipulative a good politician can be, to the point where they murder somebody because they get his name wrong, rather like that paediatrician who was attacked some years ago because everyone thought he was a paedophile. I think it would have been very interesting for the groundlings to have watched that scene.

7. Mark Antony played by Gary Oliver in David Farr's 2004 production at the RSC's Swan Theatre. Using film techniques, Antony's face was repeated on stage, and on screen '[y]ou create about a hundred Antonys receding into the distance, and that created an extraordinary, completely accidental quality'.

DF: That's a good question. Sometimes with the more well-known set pieces there is a sort of pressure to shed new light on them. But I had a particular interest in media emphasis, the way in which transmission of information is manipulated, which is clearly what Antony is doing. So in our production Antony is filmed as he gives the speech and the image of him giving the speech is then projected behind him onto the screen, so you get a double image of him on screen and live. But also, rather bizarrely and because of a curious piece of chance, the camera is actually filming him but also happens to light upon the screen upon which his image is being projected. So you create what is called an infinite image of the man's face, because the camera is filming a projection of its own image. You create about a hundred Antonys receding into the distance, and that created an extraordinary, completely accidental quality which we found in rehearsal when we were playing with the video cameras. That resonated in a way that was very powerful and as soon as that happened I knew that that would visually be the centrepiece of the speech, and then it was for the actor to explore the strange mixture of honesty and dishonesty that's in that speech.

Is the scene with Caesar's Ghost particularly problematic?

EH: No. I think ghosts in Shakespeare are never problematic, they always have an action and a reason: ghosts visiting the living, they are a portent of what is going to happen. I think as long as you don't try and make them spooky you are okay. The tent scene is such a beautiful scene. The boy sings to Brutus and it's calm and then slowly the atmosphere changes and suddenly the Ghost of Caesar appears and warns Brutus about Philippi. Ian Hogg just walked on stage – we put body make-up on him, and Ben Ormerod lit it beautifully – and it becomes an expression of the inner fear and turmoil of the person who sees the Ghost.

DF: No, because we demystified it completely. He literally just walked on and sat next to him in the tent: un-supernatural, real and strangely effective. It shone better than big shards of light and music would have done, but that is just the way we did it in our production, that suited our style. Our style was basically an honest style all the way through the piece and the honesty of that suited our production.

LB: Elizabethans believed that ghosts were not wispy things that float, but concrete – literally the corpse would come out of its grave. Greg Hicks, who played Caesar, was interested in pursuing something more demonic, but we came back to this more simple approach. In addition we had Caesar's widow, Calpurnia, dressed in black with a black veil over her face, lead his bleeding corpse into Brutus' tent. I wanted to remind the audience of this woman who otherwise has disappeared from the play, placing her personal grief as another consequence of their crime. By bringing her on stage it suggested that her rage and lament at losing her man is telepathically in sync with Brutus' guilt and grief.

Is the transition from the political first half of the play to the military second half difficult to achieve?

EH: I didn't have an interval. My production was probably quite different to other productions; it was two hours fifteen minutes straight through, so as Rome burned the mob turned into marching soldiers whilst music hammered out and they sang and then at the end of that sequence there was Cassius standing in front of his army. It was continuous. In the latter part of the play I binned all those ludicrous people who Shakespeare gets to run on obsessively and commit suicide, who you've never met before and who you don't care about. I think some of them were a result of Shakespeare being seduced by the excesses of Plutarch ... It was a straight-through show with no interval so I didn't even notice the join at all.

DF: That is why the modern setting works so well. We emphasized it. The first half took place in a strongly inner-city civilian environment, men in suits, coffee cups; we revealed the language of modernity, often in an ordinary way. And then suddenly of course to transfer that across into a war erupting is something that we all know happens. Rome at that time was not exactly a fledgling state, but it had a vulnerability about it, it was still discovering what it was, so we used as a source a nation state which was relatively young; we explored Ukraine and Georgia and states where there was a fragility inherent within the nation. That was useful, but I would say that is still true of America now, and true of much of the world still: there is an inherent uncertainty about what the nation is and what it should stand for.

LB: When I first read the play it was very clear how tricky the second half could be, as from big solid scenes the play becomes a series of fragmented skirmishes. My first thought was to perform the play without an interval simply to keep up the furious pace and horrifying escalation of violence. I also remember telling myself that the key to the play would be to give as much weight and time to the military scenes and not to rush them, or cut them. The technique of duplicating the stage action with the projected images really helped to flesh out the imagination of these scenes. Our soundscape was as huge, repetitive and unrelenting as the gesture world on stage.

One of the important strands of research was the story of Romulus and Remus founding Rome. As the story goes, these twins, who according to legend were raised by a she-wolf, fought each other to the death over a piece of land. For me this became the key to this piece: Rome was founded in bloodshed. This one act is followed by an endless saga of slaughter in the name of Rome: from the twins fighting it out on a lonely hillside to the vast field of blood that is the Empire. So in my staging as a prologue to the show, Romulus kills Remus and the first blood is spilt. We repeated the manner of this savage and primal killing in the battle scenes where the soldiers, having begun in formation, disintegrate into bestial violence.

What did you make of the roles of the wives (and more locally of the odd detail of the double reporting of Portia's suicide)?

EH: Both the women in the play know exactly what is going on with their men. Calpurnia dreams about what is going to happen to

Caesar and tells him not to go to the Senate. It is a wonderful chapter of this story: you have got a man who knows he is going to be murdered but that is not going to stop him going to the Senate because he is Caesar, and who are they to stand up against him? If he didn't go, he wouldn't be Caesar. He does talk about himself in the third person a lot, and so Calpurnia helps you understand the personal versus the public. I think Portia's scene also does a few things: it underlines what a mess Brutus is in. There is this extraordinary moment where she stabs herself in the thigh. Of course, that is quite a Catholic piece of iconography: Christ's wound in the side upon the cross, bleeding and dripping into the cup that became the Holy Grail. So it's a very powerful image to the audience of the day; today I think it tells you that this woman is falling apart, she is so frustrated and she feels her husband's pain so intensely. She wants to prove to her husband that she can bear the pain of whatever it is that he is not telling her. Those two relationships give you a little more personal, domestic insight into the hearts and minds of the two major protagonists of the play, Brutus and Caesar, and I think without the women the play would be a much drier experience to watch.

DF: I found that difficult because it is something that has changed with time. We looked at Eastern Europe, which is still an unbelievably male world, and that was helpful. Putin's wife is a perfect example of someone who never ever comes out into the limelight and is constantly behind closed doors. The reason why I found it difficult is that actresses just do not get as good a role as actors. For a while I explored having female conspirators, but then of course one of the difficulties is that there is talk of women and men in the play, so if Portia is to say what she says about a woman and then there is a female conspirator it doesn't make sense. So in the end the only other women I allowed myself were aides, political aides, messengers. I used women a lot for that, that was quite enjoyable, but we basically created a glass ceiling within a society and they weren't allowed above a certain level. Out of a genuine desire to give female actors great roles you can unfortunately contravene basic principles of the play, whether it be Lear with his three daughters, where you can't have women charging around the play in other roles. You'd have to completely subvert it, which would be very exciting at some point. To have a completely female leader...there is clearly a scope for that somewhere.

We felt [the double reporting of Portia's suicide] was very clear: when Brutus reveals to Cassius that he knows about the death there is a deeply honest moment between the two men, which is clearly because of what they have just been through in the row together, and then when the other two men come in Brutus, in the Stoic tradition, fakes ignorance of it in order that he may show us the truly Stoic reaction, which is untrue, in order to keep the morale of his men high. When Messala tells him that she is dead he replies, 'We all die, we must all die'; that is the Stoic reaction that he knows people are expecting from him, and it is important that he gives it to them at a time of potentially low morale amongst the army. The reality is completely different and it is a brilliant piece of writing.

LB: There are only two named female parts in *Julius Caesar*. Both are brilliantly portrayed. Portia: proud, aristocratic, daughter of the republican Cato, married to Brutus, the talented statesman and descendent of the liberator of Rome; and Calpurnia, equally proud and high class, but an army wife, used to her husband's long absences and to his obstinacy. Both are strong persuasive women who love their husbands and are loved back. The scenes are cleverly placed to allow us to glimpse the domestic man behind the political front. In Brutus' case it's only when he is alone with Portia that we perceive his immense capacity for tenderness, and also witness the terrible strain and inner turmoil that has taken place since he was asked to join the conspiracy.

During our early rehearsals we explored their relationship as soulmates, as twins, utterly dependent and deeply entwined with each other. This informed the scene, making it clear that any denial of each other would cause internal harm. Portia's instability and fear of abandonment is already discernable in their first scene together, and anticipates her suicide, two year later. This reading of their

8. Brutus (Sam Troughton) and Portia (Hannah Young) in Lucy Bailey's 2009–10 production for the RSC at The Courtyard Theatre: 'In Brutus' case it is only when he is alone with Portia that we perceive his immense capacity for tenderness...we explored their relationship as soulmates, as twins, utterly dependent and deeply entwined with each other.'

marriage influenced our decision to keep the two consecutive reports of her death. The first time we hear of her death is when a distraught Brutus confides the terrible news to Cassius. It's a deeply moving moment between the two men, following on from their violent quarrel. It is followed straight away by the arrival of one of their generals who delivers the news to Brutus. He pretends that this is the first time he has heard it, and reacts with Stoic fortitude that impresses the soldiers. It's a piece of public display, and hints at a growing madness in Brutus.

Did the little scene of the lynching of Cinna the Poet seem to you especially significant – given that Shakespeare was a poet?

EH: Yes. Cinna the Poet represents the free thinker, somebody apolitical, so I think it significant. It is always significant when Shakespeare writes about poets because he is writing about half of his mates, the people who would be watching and himself. Sean Hannaway was hung upside down over the stage by one foot – once they'd murdered him they strung him up and he then hung upside down over the next scene while Octavius, Lepidus and Mark Antony planned who was going to die and who was going to live; he trained for six weeks to do that – because he was upside down all the blood was rushing to his head – but it was an image taken from Mussolini's death, that famous picture of Mussolini hanging upside down, and that was quite visually striking. That whole section is really important to me because it shows in microcosm the kind of madness that can take over a large group of people when their blood is up. Let me make this analogy: it's the same kind of atmosphere that George W. Bush created with his 'you are either for them or against them' culture. 'If you are not for me, you are against me so that makes you for the terrorists and Al-Qaeda.' You couldn't discuss with Bush or Blair what they were doing because if you did the inference was that you were anti-patriotic. That's very dangerous. That's the kind of fever that those two whipped up, and it's the kind of fever that was whipped up when Cinna the Poet was murdered, and it's the kind of fever that was whipped up in Cade's revolt in *Henry VI* where they search out anybody that can read and write: 'The first thing we do, let's kill all the lawyers', which always gets a big laugh, and then they murder the Clerk of Chatham because he can read.

DF: Yes. It is one of those talismanic scenes in Shakespeare. He is very good at writing those scenes where the small character who you never see again gains enormous significance, and we placed huge amounts of significance on him in the first scene of our second half. They strung him up to this factory structure and left him hanging there, like a hung-up corpse in an old abattoir, and he stayed there throughout the whole next scene, just hanging there. We even gave him a strange, morbid song after his death, so he was an important talisman in our production.

LB: The significance of Cinna's death is that it is a terrifying piece of arbitrary violence inflicted on a civilian. It is made the more poignant because Cinna is an artist, who deals with words not blows. Mark Antony's speech unleashes mob hysteria, which leads to riots, killings and the burning of Rome. Cinna's death is the turning point in the play. Thousands more ordinary men and women will be cruelly slaughtered in the name of revenge.

SHAKESPEARE'S CAREER
IN THE THEATRE

BEGINNINGS

William Shakespeare was an extraordinarily intelligent man who was born and died in an ordinary market town in the English Midlands. He lived an uneventful life in an eventful age. Born in April 1564, he was the eldest son of John Shakespeare, a glovemaker who was prominent on the town council until he fell into financial difficulties. Young William was educated at the local grammar in Stratford-upon-Avon, Warwickshire, where he gained a thorough grounding in the Latin language, the art of rhetoric and classical poetry. He married Ann Hathaway and had three children (Susanna, then the twins Hamnet and Judith) before his twenty-first birthday: an exceptionally young age for the period. We do not know how he supported his family in the mid-1580s.

Like many clever country boys, he moved to the city in order to make his way in the world. Like many creative people, he found a career in the entertainment business. Public playhouses and professional full-time acting companies reliant on the market for their income were born in Shakespeare's childhood. When he arrived in London as a man, sometime in the late 1580s, a new phenomenon was in the making: the actor who is so successful that he becomes a 'star'. The word did not exist in its modern sense, but the pattern is recognizable: audiences went to the theatre not so much to see a particular show as to witness the comedian Richard Tarlton or the dramatic actor Edward Alleyn.

Shakespeare was an actor before he was a writer. It appears not to have been long before he realized that he was never going to grow into a great comedian like Tarlton or a great tragedian like Alleyn. Instead, he found a role within his company as the man who patched up old plays, breathing new life, new dramatic twists, into tired repertory pieces. He paid close attention to the work of the university-educated dramatists who were writing history plays and tragedies for the public stage in a style more ambitious, sweeping and poetically grand than anything which had been seen before. But he may also have noted that what his friend and rival Ben Jonson would call 'Marlowe's mighty line' sometimes faltered in the mode of comedy. Going to university, as Christopher Marlowe did, was all well and good for honing the arts of rhetorical elaboration and classical allusion, but it could lead to a loss of the common touch. To stay close to a large segment of the potential audience for public theatre, it was necessary to write for clowns as well as kings and to intersperse the flights of poetry with the humour of the tavern, the privy and the brothel: Shakespeare was the first to establish himself early in his career as an equal master of tragedy, comedy and history. He realized that theatre could be the medium to make the national past available to a wider audience than the elite who could afford to read large history books: his signature early works include not only the classical tragedy *Titus Andronicus* but also the sequence of English historical plays on the Wars of the Roses.

He also invented a new role for himself, that of in-house company dramatist. Where his peers and predecessors had to sell their plays to the theatre managers on a poorly-paid piecework basis, Shakespeare took a percentage of the box-office income. The Lord Chamberlain's Men constituted themselves in 1594 as a joint stock company, with the profits being distributed among the core actors who had invested as sharers. Shakespeare acted himself – he appears in the cast lists of some of Ben Jonson's plays as well as the list of actors' names at the beginning of his own collected works – but his principal duty was to write two or three plays a year for the company. By holding shares, he was effectively earning himself a royalty on his work, something no author had ever done before in England. When the Lord Chamberlain's Men collected their fee for performance at court in the Christmas season of 1594, three of them went along to the Treasurer of the Chamber: not just Richard Burbage the tragedian and Will Kempe the clown, but also Shakespeare the scriptwriter. That was something new.

The next four years were the golden period in Shakespeare's career, though overshadowed by the death of his only son Hamnet, aged eleven, in 1596. In his early thirties and in full command of both his poetic and his theatrical medium, he perfected his art of comedy, while also developing his tragic and historical writing in new ways. In 1598, Francis Meres, a Cambridge University graduate with his finger on the pulse of the London literary world, praised Shakespeare for his excellence across the genres:

> As Plautus and Seneca are accounted the best for comedy and tragedy among the Latins, so Shakespeare among the English is the most excellent in both kinds for the stage; for comedy, witness his *Gentlemen of Verona*, his *Errors*, his *Love Labours Lost*, his *Love Labours Won*, his *Midsummer Night Dream* and his *Merchant of Venice*: for tragedy his *Richard the 2*, *Richard the 3*, *Henry the 4*, *King John*, *Titus Andronicus* and his *Romeo and Juliet*.

For Meres, as for the many writers who praised the 'honey-flowing vein' of *Venus and Adonis* and *Lucrece*, narrative poems written when the theatres were closed due to plague in 1593–94, Shakespeare was marked above all by his linguistic skill, by the gift of turning elegant poetic phrases.

PLAYHOUSES

Elizabethan playhouses were 'thrust' or 'one-room' theatres. To understand Shakespeare's original theatrical life, we have to forget about the indoor theatre of later times, with its proscenium arch and curtain that would be opened at the beginning and closed at the end of each act. In the proscenium arch theatre, stage and auditorium are effectively two separate rooms: the audience looks from one world into another as if through the imaginary 'fourth wall' framed by the proscenium. The picture-frame stage, together with the elaborate scenic effects and backdrops beyond it, created the illusion of a self-contained world – especially once nineteenth-century developments in the control of artificial lighting meant that the auditorium could be darkened and the spectators made to focus on the lighted stage. Shakespeare, by contrast, wrote for a bare platform stage with a standing audience gathered around it in a courtyard in full daylight. The audience were always conscious of themselves and their fellow-spectators, and they shared the same 'room' as the actors. A sense of immediate presence and the creation of rapport with the audience were all-important. The actor could not afford to imagine he was in a closed world, with silent witnesses dutifully observing him from the darkness.

Shakespeare's theatrical career began at the Rose Theatre in Southwark. The stage was wide and shallow, trapezoid in shape, like a lozenge. This design had a great deal of potential for the theatrical equivalent of cinematic split-screen effects, whereby one group of characters would enter at the door at one end of the tiring-house wall at the back of the stage and another group through the door at the other end, thus creating two rival tableaux. Many of the battle-heavy and faction-filled plays that premiered at the Rose have scenes of just this sort.

At the rear of the Rose stage, there were three capacious exits, each over ten feet wide. Unfortunately, the very limited excavation of a fragmentary portion of the original Globe site, in 1989, revealed nothing about the stage. The first Globe was built in 1599 with similar proportions to those of another theatre, the Fortune, albeit that the former was polygonal and looked circular, whereas the latter was rectangular. The building contract for the Fortune survives and allows us to infer that the stage of the Globe was probably substantially wider than it was deep (perhaps forty-three feet wide and twenty-seven feet deep). It may well have been tapered at the front, like that of the Rose.

The capacity of the Globe was said to have been enormous, perhaps in excess of three thousand. It has been conjectured that about eight hundred people may have stood in the yard, with two thousand or more in the three layers of covered galleries. The other 'public' playhouses were also of large capacity, whereas the indoor Blackfriars theatre that Shakespeare's company began using in 1608 – the former refectory of a monastery – had overall internal dimensions of a mere forty-six by sixty feet. It would have made for a much more intimate theatrical experience and had a much smaller capacity, probably of about six hundred people. Since they paid at least sixpence a head, the Blackfriars attracted a more select or 'private' audience. The atmosphere would have been closer to that of an indoor performance before the court in the Whitehall Palace or at Richmond. That Shakespeare always wrote for indoor production at court as well as outdoor performance in the public theatre should make us cautious about inferring, as some scholars have, that the opportunity provided by the intimacy of the Blackfriars led to a significant change towards a 'chamber' style in his last plays – which, besides, were performed at both the Globe and the Blackfriars. After the occupation of the Blackfriars a five-act structure seems to have become more important to Shakespeare. That was because of artificial lighting: there were musical interludes between the acts, while the candles were trimmed and replaced. Again, though, something similar must have been necessary for indoor court performances throughout his career.

Front of house there were the 'gatherers' who collected the money from audience members: a penny to stand in the open-air yard, another penny for a place in the covered galleries, sixpence for the prominent 'lord's rooms' to the side of the stage. In the indoor 'private' theatres, gallants from the audience who fancied making themselves part of the spectacle sat on stools on the edge of the stage itself. Scholars debate as to how widespread this practice was in the public theatres such as the Globe. Once the audience were in place and the money counted, the gatherers were available to be extras on stage. That is one reason why battles and crowd scenes often come later rather than early in Shakespeare's plays. There was no formal prohibition upon performance by women, and there certainly were women among the gatherers, so it is not beyond the bounds of possibility that female crowd members were played by females.

The play began at two o'clock in the afternoon and the theatre had to be cleared by five. After the main show, there would be a jig – which consisted not only of dancing, but also of knockabout comedy (it is the origin of the farcical 'afterpiece' in the eighteenth-century theatre). So the time available for a Shakespeare play was about two and a half hours, somewhere between the 'two hours' traffic' mentioned in the prologue to *Romeo and Juliet* and the 'three hours' spectacle' referred to in the preface to the 1647 Folio of Beaumont and Fletcher's plays. The prologue to a play by Thomas Middleton refers to a thousand lines as 'one hour's words', so the likelihood is that about two and a half thousand, or a maximum of three thousand lines made up the performed text. This is indeed the length of most of Shakespeare's comedies, whereas many of his tragedies and histories are much longer, raising the possibility that he wrote full scripts, possibly with eventual publication in mind, in the full knowledge that the stage version would be heavily cut. The short Quarto texts published in his lifetime – they used to be called 'Bad' Quartos – provide fascinating evidence as to the kind of cutting that probably took place. So, for instance, the First Quarto of *Hamlet* neatly merges two occasions when Hamlet is overheard, the 'Fishmonger' and the 'nunnery' scenes.

The social composition of the audience was mixed. The poet Sir John Davies wrote of 'A thousand townsmen, gentlemen and whores, / Porters and servingmen' who would 'together throng' at the public playhouses. Though moralists associated female play-going with adultery and the sex trade, many perfectly respectable citizens' wives were regular attendees. Some, no doubt, resembled the modern groupie: a story attested in two different sources has one citizen's wife making a post-show assignation with Richard Burbage and ending up in bed with Shakespeare – supposedly eliciting from the latter the quip that William the Conqueror was before Richard III. Defenders of theatre liked to say that by witnessing the comeuppance of villains on the stage, audience members would repent of their own wrongdoings, but the reality is that most people went to the theatre then, as they do now, for entertainment more than moral edification. Besides, it would be foolish to suppose that audiences behaved in a homogeneous way: a pamphlet of the 1630s tells of how two men went to see *Pericles* and one of them laughed while the other wept. Bishop John Hall complained that people went to church for the same reasons that they went to the theatre: 'for company, for custom, for recreation ... to feed his eyes or his ears ... or perhaps for sleep'.

Men-about-town and clever young lawyers went to be seen as much as to see. In the modern popular imagination, shaped not least by *Shakespeare in Love* and the opening sequence of Laurence Olivier's

Henry V film, the penny-paying groundlings stand in the yard hurling abuse or encouragement and hazelnuts or orange peel at the actors, while the sophisticates in the covered galleries appreciate Shakespeare's soaring poetry. The reality was probably the other way round. A 'groundling' was a kind of fish, so the nickname suggests the penny audience standing below the level of the stage and gazing in silent open-mouthed wonder at the spectacle unfolding above them. The more difficult audience members, who kept up a running commentary of clever remarks on the performance and who occasionally got into quarrels with players, were the gallants. Like Hollywood movies in modern times, Elizabethan and Jacobean plays exercised a powerful influence on the fashion and behaviour of the young. John Marston mocks the lawyers who would open their lips, perhaps to court a girl, and out would 'flow / Naught but pure Juliet and Romeo'.

THE ENSEMBLE AT WORK

In the absence of typewriters and photocopying machines, reading aloud would have been the means by which the company got to know a new play. The tradition of the playwright reading his complete script to the assembled company endured for generations. A copy would then have been taken to the Master of the Revels for licensing. The theatre book-holder or prompter would then have copied the parts for distribution to the actors. A partbook consisted of the character's lines, with each speech preceded by the last three or four words of the speech before, the so-called 'cue'. These would have been taken away and studied or 'conned'. During this period of learning the parts, an actor might have had some one-to-one instruction, perhaps from the dramatist, perhaps from a senior actor who had played the same part before, and, in the case of an apprentice, from his master. A high percentage of Desdemona's lines occur in dialogue with Othello, of Lady Macbeth's with Macbeth, Cleopatra's with Antony and Volumnia's with Coriolanus. The roles would almost certainly have been taken by the apprentice of the lead actor, usually Burbage, who delivers the majority of the cues. Given that apprentices lodged with their masters, there would have been

9. Hypothetical reconstruction of the interior of an Elizabethan playhouse during a performance.

ample opportunity for personal instruction, which may be what made it possible for young men to play such demanding parts.

After the parts were learned, there may have been no more than a single rehearsal before the first performance. With six different plays to be put on every week, there was no time for more. Actors, then, would go into a show with a very limited sense of the whole. The notion of a collective rehearsal process that is itself a process of discovery for the actors is wholly modern and would have been incomprehensible to Shakespeare and his original ensemble. Given the number of parts an actor had to hold in his memory, the forgetting of lines was probably more frequent than in the modern theatre. The book-holder was on hand to prompt.

Backstage personnel included the property man, the tire-man who oversaw the costumes, call-boys, attendants and the musicians, who might play at various times from the main stage, the rooms above and within the tiring-house. Scriptwriters sometimes made a nuisance of themselves backstage. There was often tension between the acting companies and the freelance playwrights from whom they purchased scripts: it was a smart move on the part of Shakespeare and the Lord Chamberlain's Men to bring the writing process in-house.

Scenery was limited, though sometimes set-pieces were brought on (a bank of flowers, a bed, the mouth of hell). The trapdoor from below, the gallery stage above and the curtained discovery-space at the back allowed for an array of special effects: the rising of ghosts and apparitions, the descent of gods, dialogue between a character at a window and another at ground level, the revelation of a statue or a pair of lovers playing at chess. Ingenious use could be made of props, as with the ass's head in *A Midsummer Night's Dream*. In a theatre that does not clutter the stage with the material paraphernalia of everyday life, those objects that are deployed may take on powerful symbolic weight, as when Shylock bears his weighing scales in one hand and knife in the other, thus becoming a parody of the figure of Justice who traditionally bears a sword and a balance. Among the more significant items in the property cupboard of Shakespeare's company, there would have been a throne (the 'chair of state'), joint stools, books, bottles, coins, purses, letters (which are brought on stage, read or referred to on about eighty occasions in the complete works), maps, gloves, a set of stocks (in which Kent is put in *King Lear*), rings, rapiers, daggers, broadswords, staves, pistols, masks and vizards, heads and skulls, torches and tapers and lanterns which served to signal night scenes on the daylit stage, a buck's head, an ass's head, animal costumes. Live animals also put in appearances, most notably the dog Crab in *The Two Gentlemen of Verona* and possibly a young polar bear in *The Winter's Tale*.

The costumes were the most important visual dimension of the play. Playwrights were paid between £2 and £6 per script, whereas Alleyn was not averse to paying £20 for 'a black velvet cloak with sleeves embroidered all with silver and gold'. No matter the period of the play, actors always wore contemporary costume. The excitement for the audience came not from any impression of historical accuracy, but from the richness of the attire and perhaps the transgressive thrill of the knowledge that here were commoners like themselves strutting in the costumes of courtiers in effective defiance of the strict sumptuary laws whereby in real life people had to wear the clothes that befitted their social station.

To an even greater degree than props, costumes could carry symbolic importance. Racial characteristics could be suggested: a breastplate and helmet for a Roman soldier, a turban for a Turk, long robes for exotic characters such as Moors, a gabardine for a Jew. The figure of Time, as in *The Winter's Tale*, would be equipped with hourglass, scythe and wings; Rumour, who speaks the prologue of *2 Henry IV*, wore a costume adorned with a thousand tongues. The wardrobe in the tiring-house of the Globe would have contained much of the same stock as that of rival manager Philip Henslowe at the Rose: green gowns for outlaws and foresters, black for melancholy men such as Jaques and people in mourning such as the Countess in *All's Well that Ends Well* (at the beginning of *Hamlet*, the prince is still in mourning black when everyone else is in festive garb for the wedding of the new king), a gown and hood for a friar (or a feigned friar like the duke in *Measure for Measure*), blue coats and tawny to distinguish the followers of rival factions, a leather apron and ruler for a carpenter (as in the opening scene of *Julius Caesar* – and in *A Midsummer Night's Dream*, where this is the only sign that Peter Quince is a carpenter), a cockle hat with staff and a pair of sandals for a pilgrim or palmer (the disguise assumed by Helen in *All's Well*), bodices and kirtles with farthingales beneath for the boys who are to be dressed as girls. A gender switch such as that of Rosalind or Jessica seems to have taken between fifty and eighty lines of dialogue – Viola does not resume her 'maiden weeds', but remains in her boy's costume to the end of *Twelfth Night* because a change would have slowed down the action at just the moment it was speeding to a climax. Henslowe's inventory also included 'a robe for to go invisible': Oberon, Puck and Ariel must have had something similar.

As the costumes appealed to the eyes, so there was music for the ears. Comedies included many songs. Desdemona's willow song, perhaps a late addition to the text, is a rare and thus exceptionally poignant example from tragedy. Trumpets and tuckets sounded for ceremonial entrances, drums denoted an army on the march. Background music could create atmosphere, as at the beginning of *Twelfth Night*, during the lovers' dialogue near the end of

The Merchant of Venice, when the statue seemingly comes to life in *The Winter's Tale*, and for the revival of Pericles and of Lear (in the Quarto text, but not the Folio). The haunting sound of the hautboy suggested a realm beyond the human, as when the god Hercules is imagined deserting Mark Antony. Dances symbolized the harmony of the end of a comedy – though in Shakespeare's world of mingled joy and sorrow, someone is usually left out of the circle.

The most important resource was, of course, the actors themselves. They needed many skills: in the words of one contemporary commentator, 'dancing, activity, music, song, elocution, ability of body, memory, skill of weapon, pregnancy of wit'. Their bodies were as significant as their voices. Hamlet tells the player to 'suit the action to the word, the word to the action': moments of strong emotion, known as 'passions', relied on a repertoire of dramatic gestures as well as a modulation of the voice. When Titus Andronicus has had his hand chopped off, he asks 'How can I grace my talk, / Wanting a hand to give it action?' A pen portrait of 'The Character of an Excellent Actor' by the dramatist John Webster is almost certainly based on his impression of Shakespeare's leading man, Richard Burbage: 'By a full and significant action of body, he charms our attention: sit in a full theatre, and you will think you see so many lines drawn from the circumference of so many ears, whiles the actor is the centre . . . .'

Though Burbage was admired above all others, praise was also heaped upon the apprentice players whose alto voices fitted them for the parts of women. A spectator at Oxford in 1610 records how the audience were reduced to tears by the pathos of Desdemona's death. The puritans who fumed about the biblical prohibition upon cross-dressing and the encouragement to sodomy constituted by the sight of an adult male kissing a teenage boy on stage were a small minority. Little is known, however, about the characteristics of the leading apprentices in Shakespeare's company. It may perhaps be inferred that one was a lot taller than the other, since Shakespeare often wrote for a pair of female friends, one tall and fair, the other short and dark (Helena and Hermia, Rosalind and Celia, Beatrice and Hero).

We know little about Shakespeare's own acting roles – an early allusion indicates that he often took royal parts, and a venerable tradition gives him old Adam in *As You Like It* and the ghost of old King Hamlet. Save for Burbage's lead roles and the generic part of the clown, all such castings are mere speculation. We do not even know for sure whether the original Falstaff was Will Kempe or another actor who specialized in comic roles, Thomas Pope.

Kempe left the company in early 1599. Tradition has it that he fell out with Shakespeare over the matter of excessive improvisation. He was replaced by Robert Armin, who was less of a clown and more of a cerebral wit: this explains the difference between such parts as Lancelet Gobbo and Dogberry, which were written for Kempe, and the more verbally sophisticated Feste and Lear's Fool, which were written for Armin.

One thing that is clear from surviving 'plots' or story-boards of plays from the period is that a degree of doubling was necessary. *2 Henry VI* has over sixty speaking parts, but more than half of the characters only appear in a single scene and most scenes have only six to eight speakers. At a stretch, the play could be performed by thirteen actors. When Thomas Platter saw *Julius Caesar* at the Globe in 1599, he noted that there were about fifteen. Why doesn't Paris go to the Capulet ball in *Romeo and Juliet*? Perhaps because he was doubled with Mercutio, who does. In *The Winter's Tale*, Mamillius might have come back as Perdita and Antigonus been doubled by Camillo, making the partnership with Paulina at the end a very neat touch. Titania and Oberon are often played by the same pair as Hippolyta and Theseus, suggesting a symbolic matching of the rulers of the worlds of night and day, but it is questionable whether there would have been time for the necessary costume changes. As so often, one is left in a realm of tantalizing speculation.

THE KING'S MAN

On Queen Elizabeth's death in 1603, the new king, James I, who had held the Scottish throne as James VI since he had been an infant, immediately took the Lord Chamberlain's Men under his direct patronage. Henceforth they would be the King's Men, and for the rest of Shakespeare's career they were favoured with far more court performances than any of their rivals. There even seem to have been rumours early in the reign that Shakespeare and Burbage were being considered for knighthoods, an unprecedented honour for mere actors – and one that in the event was not accorded to a member of the profession for nearly three hundred years, when the title was bestowed upon Henry Irving, the leading Shakespearean actor of Queen Victoria's reign.

Shakespeare's productivity rate slowed in the Jacobean years, not because of age or some personal trauma, but because there were frequent outbreaks of plague, causing the theatres to be closed for long periods. The King's Men were forced to spend many months on the road. Between November 1603 and 1608, they were to be found at various towns in the south and Midlands, though Shakespeare probably did not tour with them by this time. He had bought a large house back home in Stratford and was accumulating other property. He may indeed have stopped acting soon after the new king took the throne. With the London theatres closed so much of the time and a large repertoire on the stocks, Shakespeare seems to have focused his energies on writing a few long and complex tragedies that could have been played on demand at court: *Othello*, *King Lear*, *Antony and Cleopatra*, *Coriolanus* and *Cymbeline* are among his longest and poetically grandest plays. *Macbeth* only survives in a shorter text, which shows signs of adaptation after Shakespeare's death. The bitterly satirical *Timon of Athens*, apparently a collaboration with Thomas Middleton that may have failed on the stage, also belongs to this period. In comedy, too, he wrote longer and morally darker works than in the Elizabethan period, pushing at the very bounds of the form in *Measure for Measure* and *All's Well that Ends Well*.

From 1608 onwards, when the King's Men began occupying the indoor Blackfriars playhouse (as a winter house, meaning that they only used the outdoor Globe in summer?), Shakespeare turned to a more romantic style. His company had a great success with a revived and altered version of an old pastoral play called *Mucedorus*. It even featured a bear. The younger dramatist John Fletcher, meanwhile, sometimes working in collaboration with Francis Beaumont, was pioneering a new style of tragicomedy, a mix of romance and royalism laced with intrigue and pastoral excursions. Shakespeare experimented with this idiom in *Cymbeline* and it was presumably with his blessing that Fletcher eventually took over as the King's Men's company dramatist. The two writers apparently collaborated on three plays in the years 1612–14: a lost romance called *Cardenio* (based on the love-madness of a character in Cervantes' *Don Quixote*), *Henry VIII* (originally staged with the title 'All is True'), and *The Two Noble Kinsmen*, a dramatization of Chaucer's 'Knight's Tale'. These were written after Shakespeare's two final solo-authored plays, *The Winter's Tale*, a self-consciously old-fashioned work dramatizing the pastoral romance of his old enemy Robert Greene, and *The Tempest*, which at one and the same time drew together multiple theatrical traditions, diverse reading and contemporary interest in the fate of a ship that had been wrecked on the way to the New World.

The collaborations with Fletcher suggest that Shakespeare's career ended with a slow fade rather than the sudden retirement supposed by the nineteenth-century Romantic critics who read Prospero's epilogue to *The Tempest* as Shakespeare's personal farewell to his art. In the last few years of his life Shakespeare certainly spent more of his time in Stratford-upon-Avon, where he became further involved in property dealing and litigation. But his London life also continued. In 1613 he made his first major London property purchase: a freehold house in the Blackfriars district, close to his company's indoor theatre. *The Two Noble Kinsmen* may have been written as late as 1614, and Shakespeare was in London on business a little over a year before he died of an unknown cause at home in Stratford-upon-Avon in 1616, probably on his fifty-second birthday.

About half the sum of his works were published in his lifetime, in texts of variable quality. A few years after his death, his fellow-actors began putting together an authorized edition of his complete *Comedies, Histories and Tragedies*. It appeared in 1623, in large 'Folio' format. This collection of thirty-six plays gave Shakespeare his immortality. In the words of his fellow-dramatist Ben Jonson, who contributed two poems of praise at the start of the Folio, the body of his work made him 'a monument without a tomb':

> And art alive still while thy book doth live
> And we have wits to read and praise to give...
> He was not of an age, but for all time!

SHAKESPEARE'S WORKS:
A Chronology

1589–91	*? Arden of Faversham* (possible part authorship)
1589–92	*The Taming of the Shrew*
1589–92	*? Edward the Third* (possible part authorship)
1591	*The Second Part of Henry the Sixth*, originally called *The First Part of the Contention betwixt the Two Famous Houses of York and Lancaster* (element of co-authorship possible)
1591	*The Third Part of Henry the Sixth*, originally called *The True Tragedy of Richard Duke of York* (element of co-authorship probable)
1591–92	*The Two Gentlemen of Verona*
1591–92 perhaps revised 1594	*The Lamentable Tragedy of Titus Andronicus* (probably co-written with, or revising an earlier version by, George Peele)
1592	*The First Part of Henry the Sixth*, probably with Thomas Nashe and others
1592/94	*King Richard the Third*
1593	*Venus and Adonis* (poem)
1593–94	*The Rape of Lucrece* (poem)
1593–1608	*Sonnets* (154 poems, published 1609 with *A Lover's Complaint*, a poem of disputed authorship)
1592–94/ 1600–03	*Sir Thomas More* (a single scene for a play originally by Anthony Munday, with other revisions by Henry Chettle, Thomas Dekker and Thomas Heywood)
1594	*The Comedy of Errors*
1595	*Love's Labour's Lost*

1595–97	*Love's Labour's Won* (a lost play, unless the original title for another comedy)
1595–96	*A Midsummer Night's Dream*
1595–96	*The Tragedy of Romeo and Juliet*
1595–96	*King Richard the Second*
1595–97	*The Life and Death of King John* (possibly earlier)
1596–97	*The Merchant of Venice*
1596–97	*The First Part of Henry the Fourth*
1597–98	*The Second Part of Henry the Fourth*
1598	*Much Ado about Nothing*
1598–99	*The Passionate Pilgrim* (20 poems, some not by Shakespeare)
1599	*The Life of Henry the Fifth*
1599	'To the Queen' (epilogue for a court performance)
1599	*As You Like It*
1599	*The Tragedy of Julius Caesar*
1600–01	*The Tragedy of Hamlet, Prince of Denmark* (perhaps revising an earlier version)
1600–01	*The Merry Wives of Windsor* (perhaps revising version of 1597–99)
1601	'Let the Bird of Loudest Lay' (poem, known since 1807 as 'The Phoenix and Turtle' (turtle-dove))
1601	*Twelfth Night, or What You Will*
1601–02	*The Tragedy of Troilus and Cressida*
1604	*The Tragedy of Othello, the Moor of Venice*
1604	*Measure for Measure*
1605	*All's Well that Ends Well*
1605	*The Life of Timon of Athens,* with Thomas Middleton
1605–06	*The Tragedy of King Lear*
1605–08	? contribution to *The Four Plays in One* (lost, except for *A Yorkshire Tragedy,* mostly by Thomas Middleton)
1606	*The Tragedy of Macbeth* (surviving text has additional scenes by Thomas Middleton)
1606–07	*The Tragedy of Antony and Cleopatra*
1608	*The Tragedy of Coriolanus*

1608	*Pericles, Prince of Tyre*, with George Wilkins
1610	*The Tragedy of Cymbeline*
1611	*The Winter's Tale*
1611	*The Tempest*
1612–13	*Cardenio*, with John Fletcher (survives only in later adaptation called *Double Falsehood* by Lewis Theobald)
1613	*Henry VIII (All is True)*, with John Fletcher
1613–14	*The Two Noble Kinsmen*, with John Fletcher

THE HISTORY BEHIND THE TRAGEDIES: A Chronology

Era/Date	Event	Location	Play
Greek myth	Trojan war	Troy	*Troilus and Cressida*
Greek myth	Theseus King of Athens	Athens	*The Two Noble Kinsmen*
c.tenth–ninth century BC?	Leir King of Britain (legendary)	Britain	*King Lear*
535–510 BC	Tarquin II King of Rome	Rome	*The Rape of Lucrece*
493 BC	Caius Martius captures Corioli	Italy	*Coriolanus*
431–404 BC	Peloponnesian war	Greece	*Timon of Athens*
17 Mar 45 BC	Battle of Munda: Caesar's victory over Pompey's sons	Munda, Spain	*Julius Caesar*
Oct 45 BC	Caesar returns to Rome for triumph	Rome	*Julius Caesar*
15 Mar 44 BC	Assassination of Caesar	Rome	*Julius Caesar*
27 Nov 43 BC	Formation of Second Triumvirate	Rome	*Julius Caesar*
Oct 42 BC	Battle of Philippi	Philippi, Macedonia	*Julius Caesar*
Winter 41–40 BC	Antony visits Cleopatra	Egypt	*Antony and Cleopatra*
Oct 40 BC	Pact of Brundisium; marriage of Antony and Octavia	Italy	*Antony and Cleopatra*
39 BC	Pact of Misenum between Pompey and the triumvirs	Campania, Italy	*Antony and Cleopatra*
39–38 BC	Ventidius defeats the Parthians in a series of engagements	Syria	*Antony and Cleopatra*

175

Era/Date	Event	Location	Play
34 BC	Cleopatra and her children proclaimed rulers of the eastern Mediterranean	Alexandria	*Antony and Cleopatra*
2 Sep 31 BC	Battle of Actium	On the coast of western Greece	*Antony and Cleopatra*
Aug 30 BC	Death of Antony	Alexandria	*Antony and Cleopatra*
12 Aug 30 BC	Death of Cleopatra	Alexandria	*Antony and Cleopatra*
Early first century AD	Cunobelinus/Cymbeline rules Britain (and dies before AD 43)	Britain	*Cymbeline*
During the reign of a fictional (late?) Roman emperor		Rome	*Titus Andronicus*
c.ninth–tenth century AD	Existence of legendary Amleth?	Denmark	*Hamlet*
15 Aug 1040	Death of Duncan I of Scotland	Bothnguane, Scotland	*Macbeth*
1053	Malcolm invades Scotland	Scotland	*Macbeth*
15 Aug 1057	Death of Macbeth	Lumphanan, Scotland	*Macbeth*
7 Oct 1571	Naval battle of Lepanto between Christians and Turks	The Mediterranean, off the coast of Greece	A context for *Othello*

FURTHER READING AND VIEWING

CRITICAL APPROACHES

Carnegie, David, *Julius Caesar*. The Shakespeare Handbooks Series (2009). Basic introduction with detailed commentary and discussion of key productions.

Dean, Leonard F., ed., *Twentieth Century Interpretations of Julius Caesar* (1968). Useful collection of early authoritative contributions.

Del Sapio Garbero, Maria, ed., *Identity, Otherness and Empire in Shakespeare's Rome* (2009). Ch. 3, 'Antony's Ring: Remediating Ancient Rhetoric on the Elizabethan Stage', discusses *Julius Caesar*.

Hamer, Mary, *William Shakespeare: Julius Caesar*. Writers and their Work series (1998). Argues the play is a critique of martial, masculine Roman culture.

Kahn, Coppélia, *Roman Shakespeare: Warrior, Wounds, and Women* (1997). Influential feminist reading; ch. 5 is on *Julius Caesar*, pp. 77–109.

Miles, Geoffrey, *Shakespeare and the Constant Romans* (1996). Analyses Roman Stoicism and Montaigne's critique of this and the way Shakespeare represents these debates onstage.

Miola, Robert, *Shakespeare's Rome* (1983). Influential study focusing on Shakespeare's changing conception of Rome and code of military honour; ch. 4 is on *Julius Caesar*, pp. 76–115.

Parker, Barbara, *Plato's Republic and Shakespeare's Rome: A Political Study of the Roman Works* (2004). Reads the plays in terms of political decline in Shakespeare's England; ch. 4 discusses *Julius Caesar*, pp. 74–91.

Ronan, Clifford, '*Antike Roman*': *Power Symbology and the Roman Play in Early Modern England 1585–1635* (1995). Traces the stage history of Roman plays.

Thomas, Vivian, *Shakespeare's Roman Worlds* (1989). Useful on background and sources; detailed discussion of *Julius Caesar* in ch. 2, pp. 40–92.

Thomas, Vivian, *Julius Caesar*. Harvester New Critical Introductions to Shakespeare (1992). Good basic introduction.

Wilson, Richard, *Julius Caesar*. Penguin Critical Studies (1992). Concise, sophisticated introduction to the play.

Wilson, Richard, ed., *Julius Caesar*. New Casebooks (2002). Scholarly, informed.

Zander, Horst, ed., *Julius Caesar: New Critical Essays* (2005). Useful, wide-ranging collection of recent essays.

THE PLAY IN PERFORMANCE

Bevington, David, and Holland, Peter (eds), *Julius Caesar* Shakespeare in Performance Series (2007). Accessible introduction plus text with accompanying CD.

David, Richard, *Shakespeare in the Theatre* (1978). Provides analysis of several key productions of the 1970s, which are obviously a little outdated, but the discussion is nonetheless useful as a way of understanding the play.

Dawson, Anthony B, *Watching Shakespeare: A Playgoers' Guide* (1988). Excellent guide for the theatregoer interested in the acting and directorial dilemmas presented by Shakespeare's plays, with a chapter on *Julius Caesar*.

Redgrave, Corin, *Julius Caesar* Actors on Shakespeare Series (2002). Perceptive personal account of three productions in which he participated as actor/director.

Ripley, John, *Julius Caesar on Stage in England and America, 1599–1973* (1980). Thorough, detailed, an invaluable resource.

Smallwood, Robert, ed., *Players of Shakespeare 4* (1998). Includes interview with John Nettles on playing Brutus.

AVAILABLE ON DVD

Julius Caesar, directed by Joseph L. Mankiewicz (1953, DVD 2006). With a star-studded cast and 4 Oscars: full of interest and works despite different acting styles of James Mason as Brutus, John Gielgud as Cassius and Marlon Brando as Mark Antony. Black and white.

Julius Caesar, directed by Herbert Wise for the BBC Shakespeare series (1979, DVD 2005). Well-spoken version with Richard Pasco a decent Brutus, Keith Michell a thrilling Mark Antony and Charles Gray a self-important Caesar.

Julius Caesar, directed by Yuli Kulakov with screenplay by Leon Garfield, *The Animated Tales* (1994, DVD 2007). Excellent cartoon version, voiced by Joss Ackland as Caesar, Hugh Quarshie as Cassius, David Robb as Brutus, and Jim Carter as Mark Antony.

REFERENCES

1 E. K. Chambers, *The Elizabethan Stage* (1923), Vol. II, p. 365.
2 Leonard Digges, in a prefatory poem to *Shakespeare's Poems* (1640).
3 *Julius Caesar: A Tragedy* (c. 1684).
4 Colley Cibber, quoted in John Ripley, *Julius Caesar on Stage in England and America 1599–1793* (1980), p. 20.
5 Quoted in Ripley, *Julius Caesar on Stage*, pp. 23–4.
6 *The London Stage*, Vol. II, p. 231.
7 Ripley, *Julius Caesar on Stage*, p. 26.
8 Quoted in Ripley, *Julius Caesar on Stage*, p. 29.
9 Quoted in David Daniell, ed., *Julius Caesar* (1998), p. 105.
10 Ripley, *Julius Caesar on Stage*, p. 78.
11 Andrea J. Nouryeh, 'Shakespeare and the Japanese Stage', *Foreign Shakespeare* (1993), p. 254.
12 Charles H. Shattuck, *Shakespeare on the American Stage* (1976), p. 146.
13 *Season* (New York), 30 December 1871.
14 *Stratford-upon-Avon Herald*, 26 April 1889.
15 *Stratford-upon-Avon Herald*, 26 April 1889.
16 Quoted in Ralph Berry, 'The Imperial Theme', *Shakespeare and the Victorian Stage* (1986), p. 155.
17 Berry, 'The Imperial Theme', p. 156.
18 *Stratford-upon-Avon Herald*, 22 April 1892.
19 *Birmingham Mail*, 26 April 1911.
20 *Daily Graphic*, 3 May 1916.
21 *Stratford-upon-Avon Herald*, 8 August 1919.
22 *Stratford-upon-Avon Herald*, 21 April 1922.
23 *Birmingham Gazette*, 20 April 1934.
24 *Birmingham Evening Despatch*, 20 April 1934.
25 *Birmingham Evening Despatch*, 20 April 1934.
26 Richard France, ed., *Orson Welles on Shakespeare* (1990), p. 103.
27 France, *Orson Welles on Shakespeare*, p. 106.
28 Ripley, *Julius Caesar on Stage*, p. 268.
29 Daniell, *Julius Caesar*, p. 112.
30 Eric Bentley, *New Republic*, 3 August 1953.
31 *Library Journal*, 15 June 1953.
32 Robert F. Willson Jr, *Shakespeare in Hollywood 1929–1956* (2000), p. 148.
33 *The Times* (London), 3 May 1950.
34 *Manchester Guardian*, 4 May 1950.
35 *Birmingham Post*, 4 May 1950.
36 *Birmingham Evening Despatch*, 30 May 1957.
37 *Financial Times*, 29 May 1957.
38 *Yorkshire Post*, 30 May 1957.
39 Rohan Quince, *Shakespeare in South Africa* (2000), p. 60.

40 Wilhelm Hortmann, *Shakespeare on the German Stage: The Twentieth Century* (1998), p. 207.

41 John Pettigrew and Jamie Portman, *Stratford: The First Thirty Years* (1985), Vol. II, p. 148.

42 Pettigrew and Portman, *Stratford: The First Thirty Years*, p. 253.

43 *Birmingham Post*, 23 March 1977.

44 *Daily Telegraph*, 24 March 1977.

45 *Guardian*, 24 March 1977.

46 Susan Willis, *The BBC Shakespeare Plays* (1991), pp. 197–8.

47 *Guardian*, 29 May 1999.

48 *Telegraph*, 28 May 1999.

49 *Independent*, 28 May 1999.

50 *Observer*, 24 April 2005.

51 *Independent*, 22 April 2005.

52 *Sunday Telegraph*, 24 April 2005.

53 Roger Warren, *Julius Caesar*, RSC programme note, 2001.

54 Tom Matheson, 'Royal Caesar', in *Julius Caesar: New Critical Essays*, ed. Horst Zander (2004).

55 Fran Thompson, 'Designing Caesar', in *Julius Caesar*, RSC Education Pack (1993).

56 Ian Hogg in interview with Diane Parkes, *Evening Mail*, 6 July 2001.

57 Anthony B. Dawson, *Watching Shakespeare: A Playgoers' Guide* (1988).

58 Ripley, *Julius Caesar on Stage*.

59 Matheson, 'Royal Caesar'.

60 T. C. Worsley, *Financial Times*, 10 April 1963.

61 Malcolm Rutherford, *Spectator*, 19 April 1963.

62 Sandra L. Williamson, ed., *Shakespearean Criticism*, Vol. 17, 1992.

63 A quote from Labour Party leader Michael Foot condoning political murder made for a minor controversy in *The Times*.

64 Roger Warren, *Shakespeare Quarterly*, Winter 1983.

65 Williamson, *Shakespearean Criticism*.

66 Better known as *Triumph of the Will*, this film by Leni Riefenstahl was a monumental piece of filmmaking and a prime example of the power of propaganda. A hypnotic account of the massive 1934 Nazi party rally in Nuremberg, it glorified Nazi pageantry and deified Adolf Hitler. It also earned her a place in film history and the status of a post-war pariah.

67 A play by Bertolt Brecht inspired by the German invasion of Poland, but set during the Thirty Years War in the late seventeenth century, stagings are invariably of a bleak, inhospitable, war-torn world.

68 Martin Dodsworth, *Times Literary Supplement*, 15 April 1983.

69 Dominique Goy-Blanquet, *Times Literary Supplement*, 17 April 1987.

70 He was Hitler's chief architect in Nazi Germany and in 1942 became the Minister of Armaments in Hitler's cabinet.

71 John Peter, *Sunday Times*, 12 April 1987.

72 Fran Thompson, 'Designing Caesar', *Julius Caesar*, RSC Education Pack (1993).

73 Alastair Macaulay, *Financial Times*, 7 August 1993.

74 David Thacker in interview with Sarah Hemming, *Independent*, 27 July 1993.

75 Thompson, 'Designing Caesar'.

76 Benedict Nightingale, *The Times* (London), 7 July 1993.

77 Benedict Nightingale, *The Times* (London), 22 October 2004.

78 Dominic Cavendish, *Daily Telegraph*, 22 October 2004.

79 Michael Billington, *Guardian*, 22 October 2004.
80 Dawson, *Watching Shakespeare*.
81 'Caesar, thou art revenged, / Even with the sword that killed thee' (5.3.46–7);
    'O Julius Caesar, thou art might yet, / Thy spirit walks abroad' (5.3.99–100);
    'Caesar, now be still: / I killed not thee with half so good a will' (5.5.55–6).
82 J. C. Trewin, *Illustrated London News*, 13 April 1968.
83 Benedict Nightingale, *New Statesman*, 12 May 1972.
84 Williamson, *Shakespearean Criticism*.
85 Richard David, *Shakespeare in the Theatre* (1978).
86 Michael Billington, *Guardian*, 13 May 1972.
87 J. M. Maguin, *Cahiers Elisabethains*, No. 32, October 1987.
88 James Rigney, 'Stage Worlds of Julius Caesar', in *Julius Caesar: New Critical
    Essays*, ed. Horst Zander (2004).
89 Ian Hogg in interview with Diane Parkes, *Evening Mail*, 6 July 2001.
90 Terry Hands, who directed *Julius Caesar* in 1987, in interview with Clare
    Colvin, *Drama*, No. 164, 1987.
91 Charles Spencer, *Daily Telegraph*, 1 November 1991.
92 Michael Coveney, *Observer*, 3 November 1991.
93 Mike Paterson, 'Julius Caesar', in *Shakespeare in Performance*, ed. Keith Parsons
    and Pamela Mason (1995).
94 Matheson, 'Royal Caesar'.
95 Michael Billington, *Guardian*, 7 July 1995.
96 A mighty female warrior, one of the Valkyries, and a heroine from the
    German epics, especially in the *Nibelungen* saga, in which she is an Icelandic
    princess.
97 Matheson, 'Royal Caesar'.
98 Peter Roberts, *Plays and Players*, June 1968.

ACKNOWLEDGEMENTS
AND PICTURE CREDITS

Preparation of '*Julius Caesar* in Performance' was assisted by a generous grant from the CAPITAL Centre (Creativity and Performance in Teaching and Learning) of the University of Warwick for research in the RSC archive at the Shakespeare Birthplace Trust.

Thanks as always to our indefatigable and eagle-eyed copy-editor Tracey Day and to Ray Addicott for overseeing the production process with rigour and calmness.

Picture research by Michelle Morton. Grateful acknowledgement is made to the Shakespeare Birthplace Trust for assistance with picture research (special thanks to Helen Hargest) and reproduction fees.

Images of RSC productions are supplied by the Shakespeare Centre Library and Archive, Stratford-upon-Avon. This Library, maintained by the Shakespeare Birthplace Trust, holds the most important collection of Shakespeare material in the UK, including the Royal Shakespeare Company's official archive. It is open to the public free of charge.

For more information see www.shakespeare.org.uk.

1. Directed by Herbert Beerbohm Tree (1898) Reproduced by permission of the Shakespeare Birthplace Trust
2. Directed by Glen Byam Shaw (1957) Angus McBean © Royal Shakespeare Company
3. Directed by Terry Hands (1987) Joe Cocks Studio Collection © Shakespeare Birthplace Trust

4. Directed by David Thacker (1993) Malcolm Davies ©
   Shakespeare Birthplace Trust
5. Directed by Trevor Nunn (1972) Reg Wilson © Royal
   Shakespeare Company
6. Directed by Edward Hall (2001) Manuel Harlan © Royal
   Shakespeare Company
7. Directed by David Farr (2004) Manuel Harlan © Royal
   Shakespeare Company
8. Directed by Lucy Bailey (2009) Ellie Kurttz © Royal Shakespeare
   Company
9. Reconstructed Elizabethan Playhouse © Charcoalblue

FROM THE ROYAL SHAKESPEARE COMPANY
AND MACMILLAN

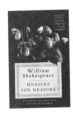   

MORE HIGHLIGHTS IN THE RSC SHAKESPEARE SERIES

AVAILABLE IN ALL GOOD BOOKSHOPS OR TO ORDER ONLINE VISIT:
www.rscshakespeare.co.uk